GOD'S HELP

for

YOUR EVERY NEED

GOD'S HELP

for

YOUR EVERY NEED

101
LIFE-CHANGING
PRAYERS

HOWARD BOOKS®
A Division of Simon & Schuster, Inc.

NEW YORK • NASHVILLE • LONDON • TORONTO • SYDNEY • NEW DELHI

Howard Books
A Division of Simon & Schuster, Inc.
1230 Avenue of the Americas
New York, NY 10020

First Howard Books hardcover edition December 2012

HOWARD and colophon are trademarks of Simon & Schuster, Inc.

For information about special discounts for bulk purchases, please contact Simon & Schuster Special Sales at 1-866-506-1949 or business@simonandschuster.com

The Simon & Schuster Speakers Bureau can bring authors to your live event. For more information or to book an event, contact the Simon & Schuster Speakers Bureau at 1-866-248-3049 or visit our website at www.simonspeakers.com.

Designed by Thinkpen Design (www.thinkpendesign.com)

Manufactured in the United States of America

10 9 8 7 6 5 4 3 2

Library of Congress Cataloging-in-Publication Data

God's help for your every need : 101 life-changing prayers.
   p. cm.
Includes index.
1. Prayers. 2. Bible—Quotations. I. Howard Books.
BV260.G53 2012
242'.8—dc23
    2012013947

ISBN 978-1-4516-9112-2
ISBN 978-1-4516-9113-9 (ebook)

CONTENTS

Attitudes and Emotions

Work and Finances

SPIRITUAL GROWTH

MY WORLD AND NATION

MISSION AND SERVICE

INTRODUCTION

YOUR INVITATION

Let us therefore come boldly to the throne of grace, that we may obtain mercy and find grace to help in time of need.

—Hebrews 4:16 NKJV

Prayer is much more than the words you say to God. Prayer goes back to the beginning of time, to the Garden of Eden, where God walked and talked with Adam and Eve daily, establishing for all to understand and see that He desires fellowship with us.

Prayer is God's invitation for us to enter into His presence with confidence, not timidity. It is His invitation to us to speak our hurts and needs and worries.

Prayer is God's antidote to the toxins of fear, cynicism, skepticism, and self-centeredness.

Prayer is the wonderful opportunity for us to grow in faith and attitude as we express our love, gratitude, and praise to God.

Prayer is the place to find forgiveness and begin repentance as we confess our sins to God.

You have been given a tremendous gift, rooted in God's desire to spend time with you. It is called prayer.

And the prayer of those who have prepared *God's Help* is that, as you respond to this gracious invitation, you would experience more fully the peace, joy, purpose, wisdom, and power of knowing God.

How to Use This Book

1. Read the Bible verses that are listed with each prayer slowly, carefully, and thoughtfully. Let the truth of God's Word pervade your thoughts and heart in order to empower your prayer time.

2. Quiet your mind from distractions before you pray. You might want to look for a place where you can shut out all noise. If your emotions and mind are still churning away, reread the Bible verses and breathe a one sentence prayer asking God to make this a time of spiritual focus.

3. Pray the prayers in this book out loud. This will give your prayer time a greater sense of the reality that you are speaking in the presence of God Almighty, the Creator of the universe, the Savior of the world. He is with you in the room.

4. The number of words we use in prayer isn't what matters. It is the sincerity of your heart and your faith that God hears and answers prayer. So repetition isn't necessary for God. However, it might be good for you. So some days you might want to pray a prayer out loud several times. You might pray some of the prayers every day for weeks and months. You might set the book aside and repeat the same prayer in your own words.

5. As you focus on the Bible verses and then speak your prayer out loud, be sure you pause and listen for God's voice. Very few people experience God's voice audibly, but countless people of faith have testified that they have heard a clear message from God as an impression in their heart.

6. Obey. As God meets you at the place of your greatest need, He will guide and direct you to acts of service; new thoughts, attitudes, and actions; areas you need to cut out of your life. Let these prayers truly be life-changing for you. This happens as you respond to God in obedience.

7. Share these prayers with others. There are times that prayer is to be solitary and other times when two or more are to gather in Jesus' name to see God's will done. Prayer is a reminder you are not alone in your needs. God is with you—and so are others who will unite with you in prayer.

8. Believe with all your heart, soul, and mind that God hears and answers your prayer. He *always* hears and answers your prayers. Some answers take time and require patience. Some answers are different than what you expected. But believe His promise that He hears your voice and answers back.

9. Season your time of prayer with praise and thanksgiving. Nothing will set your heart and mind right more quickly and fully than to recognize your true relationship with God. He is worthy of all glory and praise.

10. Extemporaneous prayers are fine, and might still be your most common form of prayer. But sometimes it is good to write down a prayer that more clearly expresses your thoughts to God. In addition to using the prayers in this book, write out some of your own prayers for specific needs. Don't know where to start? Find a scripture that means a lot to you and let that be the thought-starter.

HOME
AND
FAMILY

Christ is the center of our home;

a guest at every meal,

a silent listener to every conversation.

—AUTHOR UNKNOWN

*The Lord watches over you. The Lord is your
safe cover at your right hand. The sun will not hurt
you during the day and the moon will not hurt you
during the night. The Lord will keep you from all that
is sinful. He will watch over your soul. The Lord will
watch over your coming and going, now and forever.*

—PSALM 121:5–7 NKJV

*"Because he loves me," says the Lord, "I will rescue him;
I will protect him, for he acknowledges my name. He will
call on me, and I will answer him; I will be with him
in trouble, I will deliver him and honor him. With long
life I will satisfy him and show him my salvation."*

—PSALM 91:14–16 NIV

*Should all the hosts of death and powers
of hell unknown put their most dreadful forms
of rage and malice on, I shall be safe, for Christ
displays superior power and guardian grace.*

—ISAAC WATTS

Protect My Family

Dear Lord,

I ask that You protect my family in all ways today. I know there are
evil forces and evil people in this world that intend to cause harm,
even to children. There are so many negative messages in our culture
that undermine the importance of a loving family. And as I look
around I see so many evidences where husbands and wives have lost
their love for each other; where parents and children show little care
for each other.

I confess that I have many fears for my family. I bring those fears
to You and ask that You replace them with trust that You care for me
and all my family members. You love families and want them to be
places of safety and love.

On behalf of my family, I express my faith in You with complete
confidence today. You care about the safety of my family. You want
good, not bad for each of us. I thank You ahead of time for guarding
our paths and turning our steps from evil. I am certain You will
protect us from all forms of harm, whether it be physical danger or
spiritual temptation.

Lord, You are my family's shield.

*Submit to one another out of reverence for Christ.
Wives, submit yourselves to your own husbands as you
do to the Lord. For the husband is the head of the wife as
Christ is the head of the church, his body, of which he is
the Savior. Now as the church submits to Christ, so also
wives should submit to their husbands in everything.
Husbands, love your wives, just as Christ loved the church
and gave himself up for her to make her holy, cleansing
her by the washing with water through the word, and to
present her to himself as a radiant church, without stain
or wrinkle or any other blemish, but holy and blameless.*

—Ephesians 5:21–27 niv

*Love must be sincere. Hate what is evil; cling
to what is good. Be devoted to one another in
love. Honor one another above yourselves.*

—Romans 12:9–10 niv

*In marriage, each partner is to be an encourager
rather than a critic, a forgiver rather than a collec-
tor of hurts, an enabler rather than a reformer.*

—H. Norman Wright and Gary J. Oliver

I Want a Better Marriage

Gracious and Loving God,

You created us to love one another and for marriage to be a special bond of love, trust, and mutual respect between a husband and wife.

I love my spouse, but I see far too many ways that we fall short of what You have planned for us. Both of us have failed to express the love, the kindness, the respect, and the words that foster a wonderful relationship. As I call to You for help to turn my marriage around, O God, I don't bring grievances and judgment against my spouse, but lay my own sins and shortcomings before You. I confess that I don't have the words, thoughts, attitude, and deeds to make my marriage better in my own strength. I need You to fill me with Your grace and wisdom that I may extend that grace and wisdom to my spouse.

With Your help, I promise to do all that is in my power to improve my marriage. I ask that You give me patience when problems don't disappear instantly or I don't get the immediate response from my spouse I was looking for. Most of all I ask that You help me love and respect my spouse as you taught us through Your love of the church.

I affirm my faith that You make all things new—and that You can transform my marriage into a relationship of love and respect and joy. Continue to bless me as I bless my spouse and marriage.

I pray all this in the blessed name of Jesus.

Let all bitterness, and wrath, and anger, and clamour, and evil speaking, be put away from you, with all malice. And be ye kind one to another, tenderhearted, forgiving one another, even as God for Christ's sake hath forgiven you.

—**EPHESIANS 4:31–32 NKJV**

Finally, be strong in the Lord and in his mighty power. Put on the full armor of God, so that you can take your stand against the devil's schemes. For our struggle is not against flesh and blood, but against the rulers, against the authorities, against the powers of this dark world and against the spiritual forces of evil in the heavenly realms.

—**EPHESIANS 6:10–12 NIV**

The proof that you love someone is not that you have warm affectionate feelings toward them. The proof is in your actions, your words, and your sacrifice, your willingness to give the best of yourself and your willingness to get nothing in return.

—**KATHERINE WALDEN**

There Is Conflict in My Home

Father in Heaven,

My house is filled with conflict. We aren't kind to each other. Instead of building each other up, we tear each other down. Our words are harsh and quarrelsome. I can hardly believe how bad it has become. Some days I'm so discouraged that I'm tempted to quit and get out of here.

You are the Creator of the universe, and when the world was completed Your first act was to create the family. I know Your will is for family members to stick together; to be loyal and affirming; to be forgiving when there is disagreement; to be a safe place that gives each family member confidence to face the challenges of life.

Forgive me for any and all damage I have done to my family— help me to humbly seek forgiveness from those I've hurt. Give me Your heart of grace so that I can forgive any sins that have been committed against me. Remove bitterness and grudges from my heart.

Even if I am the only one in my family that is committed to bringing grace to my home, I thank You for the strength and boldness to become an agent for change in my family. Thank You that You are speaking to other family members right now and that change is on the way.

I will walk in Your kindness, mercy, and forgiveness this day.

I pray this in the name of the Lord.

*Fix these words of mine in your hearts and minds. . . .
Teach them to your children, talking about them when
you sit at home and when you walk along the road, when
you lie down and when you get up. Write them on the
doorframes of your houses and on your gates, so that
your days and the days of your children may be many in
the land the Lord swore to give your ancestors, as many
as the days that the heavens are above the earth.*
—DEUTERONOMY 11:18–21 NIV

*Let me set this before you as plainly as I can. If a person
climbs over or through the fence of a sheep pen instead of
going through the gate, you know he's up to no good—a
sheep rustler! The shepherd walks right up to the gate.
The gatekeeper opens the gate to him and the sheep recognize his voice. He calls his own sheep by name and
leads them out. When he gets them all out, he leads
them and they follow because they are familiar with
his voice. They won't follow a stranger's voice but will
scatter because they aren't used to the sound of it.*
—JOHN 10:1–5 THE MESSAGE

*Children are like wet cement. Whatever
falls on them makes an impression.*
—DR. HAIM GINOTT

GUARD MY CHILDREN
FROM BAD INFLUENCES

Dear Lord Almighty,

I can't keep up with all the ways that our spiritual enemy, Satan, tries to spiritually shipwreck our children. He sneaks into their lives with sinful thoughts at school, through television, through Internet, through friendships.

More than a nice home and a good education, I want to give my children the gift of knowing You. I want to bless them in many ways, but most importantly, I want them experience the joy of salvation.

Grant me wisdom to know how much freedom and how much protection to give my children. Grant me the grace to be a model of what I want them to experience. When they are in the world and there are bad influences that I can't protect them from directly, I pray that they will remember my words of counsel and know how much they are loved by me. I affirm my belief that they will experience Your words and Your love in such a strong way that they won't be turned toward evil.

You are the Good Shepherd and You drive away wild animals from Your flock. I pray that You would do that for my children today.

I pray this with thanksgiving for Your kindness to me.

Be well balanced (temperate, sober of mind),
be vigilant and cautious at all times; for that enemy of
yours, the devil, roams around like a lion roaring [in fierce
hunger], seeking someone to seize upon and devour.
—1 PETER 5:8 AMP

I have learned how to be content
(satisfied to the point where I am not disturbed
or disquieted) in whatever state I am.
—PHILIPPIANS 4:11 AMP

So be sure when you step, step with
care and great tact. And remember that
life's a great balancing act.
—DR. SEUSS

I Need to Find Balance

Dear God Who Guides,

I have let my life get out of balance. The relationship between work, rest, play, family, worship, and service is not right. I am trapped by unhealthy attention in some areas of life and a lack of attention to some things that really matter to me—and to You.

I know that if I seek You and Your kingdom first, if I make You the number one priority in my life, the rest of my activities will fall into place. So I do declare my love and devotion to You right now.

I also need Your guidance on establishing priorities and organizing my life. I ask that You would begin to speak Your words of direction into my heart and mind right now. If You have already been telling me where I need more and less focus and I haven't listened, I open my ears to Your voice right now.

I thank You that You have drawn me to You through prayer. My life already feels more in alignment with Your will—just through expressing these simple words of faith.

I do pray this with love and faith—and in Jesus' name.

Show us Your mercy, Lord, and grant us Your sal-
vation. I will hear what God the Lord will speak,
for He will speak peace to His people and to His
saints; but let them not turn back to folly.

—PSALM 85:7–9 NKJV

And afterward, I will pour out my Spirit on all people.
Your sons and daughters will prophesy, your old men will
dream dreams, your young men will see visions. . . .
And everyone who calls on the name of the Lord
will be saved; for on Mount Zion and in Jerusa-
lem there will be deliverance, as the Lord has said,
even among the survivors whom the Lord calls.

—JOEL 2:28,32 NIV

No man is excluded from calling upon God, the
gate of salvation is set open unto all men: neither
is there any other thing which keepeth us back
from entering in, save only our own unbelief.

—JOHN CALVIN

Bring My Loved One to Salvation

Dear Savior God,

Thank You for the gift of salvation, for making me a new person through the blood of Jesus Christ. And I thank You that You have put Your love in my heart so that I see and love others as You do.

I don't stand in judgment of others. Only You know the heart of men and women, boys and girls. But there are people in my life who I know have not asked You to forgive them for their sins and have not asked You to be Lord of their lives. I am thinking of a family member in particular right now—and I bring that person to You.

In faith, I ask that You speak directly to my family member's heart and mind. You know exactly the areas of pride and resistance that keep them from opening themselves to You. I pray You would break down those barriers in their heart. Let my life be a witness to the joy of salvation. If there are words of grace and mercy I can speak into their life, I pray that You would impress them in my mind. When I need to hold my tongue and remain silent so they can hear Your voice, I pray for that wisdom.

I pray they would receive Your gift of eternal life in the gracious name of Jesus.

*Therefore a man shall leave his father
and his mother and hold fast to his wife,
and they shall become one flesh.*

—GENESIS 2:24 ESV

*Delight yourself in the Lord, and he will
give you the desires of your heart.*

—PSALM 37:4 ESV

*What you are as a single person, you will be as a
married person, only to a greater degree. Any negative
character trait will be intensified in a marriage relationship, because you will feel free to let your guard
down—that person has committed himself to you and
you no longer have to worry about scaring him off.*

—JOSH MCDOWELL

I Want to Be Married

God of Love,

I know that I don't have to be married to be a complete, whole, and happy person. I know it is better to be single than to marry the wrong kind of person. I know that You love me and have a perfect plan for my life. But You already know how much I want to find the perfect mate for me and be married for life.

I ask that, even as I hope to find the right person for me, You will help me to become the right person for someone else. Help me to be a person of character and kindness. Help me to be the kind of person who will help foster a faithful marriage and a joyful home. If there are areas of my personality and life that need to be refined, I ask that You do that work in me.

You know how badly I want to be married, but I pray that You would protect me from settling for the wrong person. I pray that I would only marry a person that shares my values and beliefs and would be as committed to me as I would be to them.

If You already have someone in mind for me, I pray that You would protect them in the same way I ask for protection. Make them into the person You want them to be and keep them from entanglements that will rob them of their esteem for marriage and the opposite sex.

I place my life and my dreams of marriage in Your hands with full trust that Your timing is always right. Thank You for putting a delight for love and marriage in my heart.

In Jesus' beautiful name.

For you created my inmost being; you knit me together in my mother's womb. I praise you because I am fearfully and wonderfully made; your works are wonderful, I know that full well. My frame was not hidden from you when I was made in the secret place, when I was woven together in the depths of the earth. Your eyes saw my unformed body; all the days ordained for me were written in your book before one of them came to be. How precious to me are your thoughts, God! How vast is the sum of them!

—**PSALM 139:13–17 NIV**

See what great love the Father has lavished on us, that we should be called children of God! And that is what we are!

—**1 JOHN 3:1 NIV**

God loves each of us as if there were only one of us.

—**SAINT AUGUSTINE**

My Child Has Low Self-Worth

Loving Father,

You know how much I love my child. And I know how much You love my child. I don't fully understand why my child is suffering from low self-worth. But You knew my child even before they were born. You know how they are knit together physically, spiritually, and emotionally.

First of all, dear God, if there is anything I am doing to hurt the self-esteem of my child that I am not conscious of, bring what I am doing to light so I will know what changes I can make. If there is anyone else inside or outside the family that is attacking their sense of self-worth, I ask that You bind them from those attacks right now.

Father, if there is a special grace, a special capacity for love and service You are developing in my child through their struggles, I pray all of us would have patience to let Your perfect work blossom in their life.

But Father, my deepest desire and prayer is that my child would know without a shadow of a doubt how much You love them and how valuable that makes them. Restore their self-worth through that confidence and knowledge.

I pray this in Jesus' matchless name.

Is anyone among you sick? Let them call the elders
of the church to pray over them and anoint them
with oil in the name of the Lord. And the prayer offered
in faith will make the sick person well; the Lord will raise
them up. If they have sinned, they will be forgiven.
—JAMES 5:14 NIV

I consider that our present sufferings are not worth
comparing with the glory that will be revealed in us.
—ROMANS 8:18 NIV

Christ shared our experience; he suffered as we suffer;
he died as we shall die, and for forty days in the desert
he underwent the struggle between good and evil.
—BASIL HUME

MY LOVED ONE IS SUFFERING PHYSICALLY

O God Who Heals,

My loved one is suffering. It hurts me in mind and spirit to see the physical pain they are experiencing.

Jesus Christ healed the blind and the lame; He cast out demons; He brought sanity to the mentally ill; He brought the dead back to life. You, O God, are the Creator and giver of life. You are the Great Physician. You are able to bring physical healing through Your command.

In Your Word, You also show us that suffering can be used for other purposes that are good and that bless both the sufferer and those around them. You can do incredible works in us and through us when we suffer.

So I bring my friend before You in faith. My will is that they be completely healed and that all pain be removed from their body. I pray this in faith, believing that You can do exactly that. I also pray with humility and trust that Your will be done. Whether there is complete healing or a special spiritual impartation or both—I know You are answering my prayer right now.

I pray this in the name of Jesus, the Great Physician.

*The fear of the Lord is the beginning of wisdom,
and knowledge of the Holy One is understanding.*

—PROVERBS 9:10 NIV

*Train up a child in the way he should go,
and when he is old he will not depart from it.*

—PROVERBS 22:6 NKJV

*Don't worry that children never listen to you;
worry that they are always watching you.*

—ROBERT FULGHUM

HELP MY CHILDREN MAKE WISE DECISIONS

Gracious Father,

My children are confronted by so many decisions every day in a variety of areas: relationship choices, entertainment choices, priority choices, and so much more. Some decisions are routine but some are loaded with future and spiritual consequences. You know some specific decisions they are facing right now that are on my heart.

Father, I commit myself to seeking Your will and making wise decisions in my own life as a good role model for my children. When I make bad decisions, I ask that You give me the grace and confidence to be honest and accountable before You and those whom I love. Father, I will also remind my children to seek Your wisdom and counsel in prayer.

I know that, as they get older, they must make more and more of their own decisions, and as much as I want to handle things myself, I will honor their need to mature with Your help. Father, I live in a society that tries to remove the consequences of decisions and with Your help I will allow my children to appropriately experience the consequences of their decisions.

My prayer right now, O Father, is that my child will trust You and know that You want what is best for their life. I pray that You would strengthen their courage to always make the right decision.

I thank You in Jesus' name.

The Lord remembers us and will bless us. . . . he will bless those who fear the Lord—small and great alike. May the Lord cause you to flourish, both you and your children. May you be blessed by the Lord, the Maker of heaven and earth.

—Psalm 115:12,14–15 niv

I am my beloved's, and my beloved is mine.

—Song of Solomon 6:3 nkjv

One of the nicest things you can say to your partner: "If I had it to do over again, I'd choose you. Again."

—Author Unknown

Bless My Spouse

Loving Father,

From the beginning of creation, You have planted in our hearts the desire for the love and intimacy that can only be found in marriage. Even if our sinful ways have damaged the reputation of marriage, deep down in our spirits, we know that You have created us for the joining of spirits and minds that can only come through the bonds of marriage.

I thank You this day for my spouse. I pray that You would nourish our bonds of love, commitment, and affection for one another. I pray that we will be graceful to each other, quick to forgive, slow to anger. I pray that You will help us to season our words with grace and kindness.

I ask a special blessing on my spouse right now. I pray that they will feel Your presence in all they do today. I pray that they will feel confidence in conversations and endeavors, knowing that they are loved by You and loved by me. If there are particular challenges and difficulties they are facing, I pray they would be strengthened from within, knowing that You are with them every step of the way.

Thank You for loving my spouse and giving them to me.

In Jesus' name.

*A new commandment I give to you, that you love
one another; as I have loved you, that you also love
one another. By this all will know that you are My
disciples, if you have love for one another.*

—JOHN 13:34–35 NKJV

*Finally, all of you, be like-minded, be sympathetic,
love one another, be compassionate and humble.
Do not repay evil with evil or insult with insult.
On the contrary, repay evil with blessing, because to this
you were called so that you may inherit a blessing.*

—1 PETER 3:8–9 NIV

*Love the family! Defend and promote it as the basic cell
of human society; nurture it as the prime sanctuary of life.*

—POPE JOHN PAUL II

I Want to Show Love to My Family

Creator God,

I confess that I am sometimes more kind and pleasant to those outside my family than inside my family. We are quarrelsome and impatient with one another. I take full responsibility for my attitudes and actions today and ask that You forgive me and work inside of me to make me a new person.

I know that You created the family to be a haven of love and support. My family knows I love them—but I am not showing it very well. I pray that You would turn my impatience into patience. I pray that, when I get wrapped up in my own thoughts, I would show active interest in my family members and become a much better listener. When I take them for granted I pray You would remind me to be grateful.

Thank You for showing all of us the full extent of Your love by laying down Your life on the Cross. That sacrifice is what has saved me from my sins and given me new life. Now I want to better and more fully express that love You have put in my heart.

Patience. Attentiveness. Humor. Kindness. Slowness to anger. I pray that even if I never said a word about knowing You, my family would know that I am a person of love by the way I treat them.

In the loving name of Jesus.

Therefore, since we have a great high priest who has ascended into heaven, Jesus the Son of God, let us hold firmly to the faith we profess. For we do not have a high priest who is unable to empathize with our weaknesses, but we have one who has been tempted in every way, just as we are—yet he did not sin. Let us then approach God's throne of grace with confidence, so that we may receive mercy and find grace to help us in our time of need.

—HEBREWS 4:14–16 NIV

Love is patient, love is kind. It does not envy, it does not boast, it is not proud. It does not dishonor others, it is not self-seeking, it is not easily angered, it keeps no record of wrongs. Love does not delight in evil but rejoices with the truth. It always protects, always trusts, always hopes, always perseveres. Love never fails.

—1 CORINTHIANS 13:4–8 NIV

It is not your love that sustains the marriage, but from now on, the marriage that sustains your love.

—DIETRICH BONHOEFFER

WE ARE HAVING MARITAL PROBLEMS

Heavenly Father,

If love and marriage were based on emotions, I don't think I could stay married. We are not doing well. We don't seem to like and love each other. We have lost the passion that we had when we made our vows before You. We find fault, argue, and then ignore each other. Some days it just doesn't seem we care to keep trying.

Father, begin a new work in our marriage, and let it begin in my heart. I pray for the same work in my spouse's heart and life, but even if it only starts with me, give me the strength to work on behalf of my marriage. You have taught us that love is patient and kind, that it is not easily angered and keeps no record of wrongs. You have taught us that love is not self-seeking and doesn't seek revenge. You have taught us that love always protects, always trusts, always hopes, always perseveres. You have taught us that love never fails.

I don't want our love—our marriage—to fail, Heavenly Father. I want us to persevere. I commit myself to doing and experiencing true love with Your help.

In the name of Jesus, who taught us what true love looks like.

*Call unto me, and I will answer thee, and show thee
great and mighty things, which thou knowest not.*

—JEREMIAH 33:3 KJV

*In the same way, the Spirit helps us in our weakness.
We do not know what we ought to pray for, but the Spirit
himself intercedes for us through wordless groans.
And he who searches our hearts knows the mind
of the Spirit, because the Spirit intercedes
for God's people in accordance with the will of God.*

—ROMANS 8:26–27 NIV

*Live so that when your children think of fairness,
caring, and integrity, they think of you.*

—H. JACKSON BROWN, JR.

My Child Is Struggling and I Don't Know How to Help

Heavenly Father,

You know what my child is going through right now. You know how much I love my child and how much I want to do something, anything, to make the situation right—but I'm helpless. There is nothing I have power to do to make things better. I don't believe this problem is something my child created, so I confess that I am feeling this isn't fair.

But You are the God of all compassion and I thank You that my child's situation matters to You. Thank You that my feelings matter to You, too. I also know that You are able to perform miracles to change situations immediately. If it be Your will, I pray that You would do that right now. I will always praise You for your miraculous acts.

I know that sometimes You don't answer exactly how we want You to—but that Your grace is sufficient for every need my child has—and every need in my life. I know that You work out all things for those who love You—and You know how much we love You.

In my heart with all faith and in Your name, I know in my heart and express with my lips that my child is whole and complete and loved by You.

In Jesus' name I pray.

And now, Master God, being the God you are,
speaking sure words as you do, and having just said
this wonderful thing to me, please, just one more thing:
Bless my family; keep your eye on them always.
You've already as much as said that you would, Master God!
Oh, may your blessing be on my family permanently!
—2 Samuel 7:28–29 The Message

The jailer brought them into his house and set a meal
before them; he was filled with joy because he had come
to believe in God—he and his whole household.
—Acts 16:34 niv

A man ought to live so that everybody knows he is a
Christian . . . and most of all, his family ought to know.
—Dwight L. Moody

I Want My Whole Family to Be Saved

Dear God Who Saves,

You placed me within the family that You chose for me, and I know that Your purpose and plan for us is far greater than I can imagine. Special privileges, responsibilities, and blessings come with being a part of a family. I don't want to love the whole world—and somehow not show that same love to my own family members.

I pray right now that You would touch the heart of any member of my family who does not know Jesus Christ as their Lord and Savior. Please send people who know You to cross their paths and remind them of Your great love. Speak directly to their spirit through the Holy Spirit who convicts of truth and sin.

Make my words effective. Provide me with opportunities to share the love You have planted in my heart. I pray that I will truly demonstrate the grace and love of a follower of Jesus Christ through my actions. Let my life be a beacon that draws them to You.

I thank You, Lord, that not one will be lost, but my whole household will rejoice together with You in eternity, for You are our redeemer.

In Jesus' mighty name.

Always keep yourselves united in the Holy Spirit,
and bind yourselves together with peace.
—EPHESIANS 4:3 NLT

Behold, how good and how pleasant it is for brethren
to dwell together in unity! . . . For there the Lord
commanded the blessing—life forevermore.
—PSALM 133:1,3 NKJV

The family should be a closely-knit group.
The home should be a self-contained shelter of security;
a kind of school where life's basic lessons are taught;
and a kind of church where God is honored;
a place where wholesome recreation and
simple pleasures are enjoyed.
—BILLY GRAHAM

I Want My Family to Live in Unity

Dear Heavenly Father,

Thank You for my family. We are not perfect—I am not perfect—but I am so blessed and feel so much gratitude for the family You have given me. I ask that You help my family to be united through the presence of the Spirit in our home. Plant a love in our hearts for one another that will overcome any difficult days ahead.

I don't come to You because there is a crisis but because I want what is good about our family to become better. There are so many broken homes today, and I want us to draw closer to one another.

If I am contributing to strife in any way, I pray that You will help me in that area of my life through Your grace and mercy. Help me to grow in my ability to speak and act with grace and poise. You know our family weaknesses and I pray that You will help us overcome those by focusing on Your love for us. Thank You for helping me to become a family member who provides my family with a sense of security and peace.

In Jesus' name.

Honor your father and your mother,
as the Lord your God has commanded you, that your days
may be long, and that it may be well with you
in the land which the Lord your God is giving you.

—**DEUTERONOMY 5:16 NKJV**

Praise the Lord, my soul; all my inmost being, praise his
holy name. Praise the Lord, my soul, and forget not all
his benefits—who forgives all your sins and heals all your
diseases, who redeems your life from the pit and crowns you
with love and compassion, who satisfies your desires with
good things so that your youth is renewed like the eagle's.

—**PSALM 103:1–5 NIV**

Just because somebody doesn't love you
the way you want them to doesn't mean they
don't love you with everything they got.

—**AUTHOR UNKNOWN**

My Parent's Health Is Deteriorating

Father God,

I thank You for my parents and all the blessings that they have provided for me.

You know the situation I have with a parent who is not doing well healthwise as they grow older. You know their physical, mental, and emotional condition.

I ask that You draw them near to You and that at this stage of life they would have a wonderful sense of Your love and presence. May the hope and promise of eternal life be a consolation in all their difficulties.

I pray also that You would guide both them and all family members so that we would make the very best decisions on treatments, living arrangements, and everything else that contributes to their health and lifestyle.

My parent has been a help to me countless times, and I pray that now I would be a help and blessing to them. Grant me the energy and grace to be all that I need to be for them at this time—and fulfill all other obligations I have in life.

I pray that there would be improvement physically and mentally so my parent feels good and can remain appropriately active.

All this I pray in the name of Jesus.

*So let us seize and hold fast and retain without
wavering the hope we cherish and confess and our
acknowledgement of it, for He Who promised is reliable
(sure) and faithful to His word. And let us consider and
give attentive, continuous care to watching over one
another, studying how we may stir up (stimulate and
incite) to love and helpful deeds and noble activities.*
—**HEBREWS 10:23–24 AMP**

*"Haven't you read," he replied, "that at the beginning the
Creator 'made them male and female,' and said,
'For this reason a man will leave his father and mother
and be united to his wife, and the two will become
one flesh'? So they are no longer two, but one flesh. Therefore
what God has joined together, let no one separate."*
—**MATTHEW 19:4 NIV**

*The secret to having a good marriage is to
understand that marriage must be total, it must
be permanent, and it must be equal.*
—**FRANK PITTMAN**

Protect Our Marital Values

God of Love,

I thank You for my spouse. They are a gift from You. You have brought us together to love one another until death do us part. I understand that no human relationship is perfect, but You can still use both our compatabilities and differences to make each of us a better person.

We do not live in a culture that always honors the promises made at the wedding altar. Many individuals have broken their promise to be faithful to their spouse. Because so many people are not committed to sexual purity, there is a lot of temptation surrounding us.

I want to be one who stands faithful and true in my promise to forsake all others and give myself only to my spouse. I want to be this kind of person for my spouse's sake, but also for my own sake and to honor You and the covenant of marriage You created. I pray that You will give me wisdom not to put myself in places and situations where infidelity would be easy. When situations are outside my control and temptation comes my way, I pray that I would flee from it, even as Joseph fled from Potiphar's wife in the book of Genesis.

I pray that I would never trade my integrity for a moment of pleasure. You are always beside me, and I thank You that You will protect and bless my commitment to purity.

In the name of Jesus.

My son, do not despise the Lord's discipline, and do not resent his rebuke, because the Lord disciplines those he loves, as a father the son he delights in.
—PROVERBS 3:11–12 NIV

Fathers, do not provoke your children to anger, but bring them up in the discipline and instruction of the Lord.
—EPHESIANS 6:4 ESV

American youngsters tend to live as if adolescence were a last fling at life rather than a preparation for it.
—AUTHOR UNKNOWN

My Child Is Belligerent

Father of Love,

My heart is just sick. I love my children so much, but they aren't reciprocating that love. They are angry and rebellious inside and outside the home. Their words are like fiery darts, and they use them to hurt me. Their hearts are hard, and they are unresponsive when I try to talk to them about how they are acting and treating others, including me.

I know there are many wonderful, gracious people who went through a season of rebellion and belligerence. I also know some people have taken the wrong path and stayed on it. I know that as miserable as my children are making me, they are equally miserable inside. I want so much for them to experience Your love and all the joys that good relationships bring in life. I also know that I can't make their choices and decisions for them.

So I ask, heavenly Father, that You give me a special outpouring of grace to not be defeated by their belligerence. I pray that their words would not injure or make me feel bad about myself. I pray also that my steadfast love for them would be a reminder of Your love for them. I pray that Your Holy Spirit would continue to speak words of grace and conviction in their heart.

In Jesus' name.

Therefore know that the Lord your God,
He is God, the faithful God who keeps covenant
and mercy for a thousand generations with those
who love Him and keep His commandments.

—DEUTERONOMY 7:9 NKJV

The righteous lead blameless lives;
blessed are their children after them.

—PROVERBS 20:7 NIV

We are told to let our light shine, and if it does,
we won't need to tell anybody it does. Lighthouses don't
fire cannons to call attention to their shining—they just shine.

—D. L. MOODY

I Want to Leave a Legacy of Faith

Dear Father in Heaven,

I know that I'm not perfect and that I won't always say and do the right thing, even with my children. Help me to have the courage and grace to apologize when it's needed.

I also know that even when I do the right thing, there might be periods of time when my children don't recognize and appreciate fully the dynamics we believe in, including discipline and discernment.

But even if I'm not perfect and my best efforts aren't always received in the way I want them to be in the moment, I still want to do all I can to be a parent of grace, wisdom, strength, and faith. As my children see me responding to Your grace by obediently searching Your Word, attending church, praying, and seasoning all my conversation with grace, I pray this will become a model and legacy for their own life.

Heavenly Father, I want to live my life so that my children know You better. I want them to be proud of me, but most of all, I want You to be proud of the person I am becoming in Your grace.

In the name of the Son.

ATTITUDES AND EMOTIONS

Believe God's word and power more than you

believe your own feelings and experiences.

—Samuel Rutherford

Are you tired? Worn out? Burned out on religion?
Come to me. Get away with me and you'll recover
your life. I'll show you how to take a real rest.
Walk with me and work with me—watch how I do it.
—**Matthew 11:28–29 The Message**

Whoever dwells in the shelter of the Most High will rest
in the shadow of the Almighty. I will say of the Lord,
"He is my refuge and my fortress, my God, in whom I trust."
—**Psalm 91:1–2 niv**

If you look at the world, you'll be distressed. If you look
within, you'll be depressed. If you look at God you'll be at rest.
—**Corrie ten Boom**

I Need Rest

O Lord,

I come to You with a sense of weariness and fatigue, both physically and emotionally. I have no energy. There are things I need to get done, and I'm just not sure how I can do it all. I don't feel like I have anything left to offer. I am weary in my soul.

I don't understand all the reasons why I can't find rest, but I lay this need before You and ask that You would act on my behalf and give me the rest I need. Help me to sleep well. When I take a break in the day, let it be a time of recharging my emotional batteries. Help me to turn my eyes toward You and not the distractions and worries that are robbing me of rest.

Thank You for inviting me to bring my burdens to You. Thank You for understanding that I sometimes get tired and struggle to positively express myself. I am humbled and grateful that You still accept and embrace me as I am, and that You offer to carry my load with me.

Lord, just knowing that You are close to me right now gives rest to my soul. I receive Your gift of rest with faith.

*There is therefore now no condemnation to those
who are in Christ Jesus, who do not walk according
to the flesh, but according to the Spirit.*

—ROMANS 8:1 NIV

*As far as the east is from the west, so far
has He removed our transgressions from us.*

—PSALM 103:12 NKJV

*We are not nearly as vigorous in appropriating God's
forgiveness as He is in extending it. Consequently, instead of
living in the sunshine of God's forgiveness through Christ,
we tend to live under an overcast sky of guilt most of the time.*

—JERRY BRIDGES

I Feel Guilty

Dear God of Forgiveness,

When I was lost and without You, You called me by name and spoke to me with words of mercy, forgiveness, and healing. You offered me new life and forgiveness, not the spiritual death and guilt I was living in. I will never forget the moment that I truly recognized for the first time how empty my life was without You.

But right now I can't shake feelings of guilt over my past sins. I know there is a good conviction that leads to repentance. But I also know that when I confess my sins, You are faithful to forgive me of all unrighteousness. I don't know why You are so loving and gracious but I know that is Your promise to me.

If there is some ongoing sin that has entangled me, I ask for forgiveness and freedom now. I receive Your spiritual provision in faith.

I know in my heart that I am united with Jesus Christ—and I pray that I will experience that in my heart and emotions as well.

In Jesus' merciful name.

Be strong and courageous. Do not be afraid or terrified because of them, for the Lord your God goes with you; he will never leave you nor forsake you.

—Deuteronomy 31:6 NIV

I lift up my eyes to the mountains—where does my help come from? My help comes from the Lord, the Maker of heaven and earth. He will not let your foot slip—he who watches over you will not slumber; indeed, he who watches over Israel will neither slumber nor sleep. The Lord watches over you— the Lord is your shade at your right hand; the sun will not harm you by day, nor the moon by night. The Lord will keep you from all harm—he will watch over your life; the Lord will watch over your coming and going both now and forevermore.

—Psalm 121 NIV

If I could hear Christ praying for me in the next room, I would not fear a million enemies. Yet distance makes no difference. He is praying for me.

—Robert Murray McCheyne

I Need Courage

Dear God,

With You on my and at my side, I know that I have absolutely nothing to fear. But there are still times when I take my eyes off You—when I forget Your promise that You will never leave me nor forsake me—and I let fear invade and take control of my life.

Right now I feel defeated by fear. I am not doing what I am supposed to in life because I am afraid of what will happen to me. I am struggling to trust You to protect and empower me. My eyes are focused on what I perceive to be threats all around me, rather than focused on You. Even before I speak it, You know the specific fear that is most plaguing my life right now.

God, I ask that You would do a work in my heart and mind that I cannot do myself. Please remove the fear that is robbing me of joy, purpose, and success. Help me to trust You as the one true source of courage. I don't claim courage through my own strength, but I do receive the courage I need for the challenges and tasks facing me from loving and trusting You.

I affirm Your promise that You never leave me nor forsake me. Thank You for the courage that comes from that trust.

*First be reconciled to your brother, and then come
and offer your gift. Agree with your adversary quickly,
while you are on the way with him, lest your adversary
deliver you to the judge, the judge hand you over
to the officer, and you be thrown into prison.*

—MATTHEW 5:24–25 NKJV

*For if you forgive other people when they sin against you,
your heavenly Father will also forgive you. But if you do not
forgive others their sins, your Father will not forgive your sins.*

—MATTHEW 6:14–15 NIV

*You will know that forgiveness has begun when you recall
those who hurt you and feel the power to wish them well.*

—LEWIS B. SMEDES

A Friend Has Betrayed Me

My Savior,

I feel angry and hurt right now. Someone I have been friends with has betrayed me. I feel a major violation of trust. I feel confusion. I feel a profound sadness. I want to cry and I want to yell.

I know that no one understands betrayal more deeply than You, O God. Jesus Christ took on the form of humanity to redeem us of our sins, and He experienced the full measure of betrayal, even from His closest friends who turned from Him in His hour of need.

I bring this situation and lay it before You. If my friend asks for forgiveness I'm not sure I feel able to do so right now, but I will obey. If they desire our relationship to continue, I ask for the wisdom to know if that is beneficial and the grace to do whatever You would have me to do.

Thank You, Savior God. You are a faithful friend in all moments of life. Thank You for guarding my heart from negativity. I pray that any anger, malice, and wrath would be removed from my heart.

In Jesus' wonderful name.

Forget the former things; do not dwell on the past.

See, I am doing a new thing! Now it springs up;

do you not perceive it? I am making a way in the

wilderness and streams in the wasteland.

—ISAIAH 43:18–19 NIV

Therefore if any man be in Christ, he is a new creature:

old things are passed away; behold, all things are become new.

—2 CORINTHIANS 5:17 KJV

Failure is a detour, not a dead-end street.

—ZIG ZIGLAR

I Feel Like a Failure

God of Grace,

I have had such high hopes for the plans I have made. But they haven't worked out. It seems like every decision I make and every direction I take is the wrong one. My confidence is at an all-time low. I feel like a failure. The reason is simple. I keep failing.

I have come to You before in need of help. I don't know why, but You always invite and welcome me into Your presence. You know exactly what is happening in my life already. You know why things aren't working out. I ask first of all that I would learn from my failures. Since I keep failing, I haven't done this very well in the past. Give me the humility and wisdom to learn what I have done wrong—and to be willing to make corrections. I also pray that You would renew a sense of optimism and enthusiasm in me so that I will get up after a fall and try again.

If there are attitudes or personality traits that are causing me to fail, I ask You to work inside me to make me a new person. I submit to Your work—and will do as You ask me.

Thank You for not looking at me as a failure, but as Your beloved child. That means the world to me and gives me hope to press on toward success. I will give You praise for anything and all I accomplish in life.

In Jesus' blessed name.

The Lord bless you and keep you; the Lord make his face shine on you and be gracious to you; the Lord turn his face toward you and give you peace.

—NUMBERS 6:24–26 NIV

One day Jesus said to his disciples, "Let us go over to the other side of the lake." So they got into a boat and set out. As they sailed, he fell asleep. A squall came down on the lake, so that the boat was being swamped, and they were in great danger. The disciples went and woke him, saying, "Master, Master, we're going to drown!" He got up and rebuked the wind and the raging waters; the storm subsided, and all was calm.

—LUKE 8:22–24 NIV

The Lord will either calm your storm . . . or allow it to rage while He calms you.

—AUTHOR UNKNOWN

I NEED PEACE

Prince of Peace,

My life and mind are in turmoil. I come to You with a deep sense of need, knowing that my heart is filled with anger, confusion, resentments, disappointment, bitterness—all the things that You called me from when You offered me the gift of salvation.

There's so much I need right now. But I begin by asking You for peace. Quiet my mind. Calm my raging emotions. Help me to stop thrashing around and muddying the waters of my life.

Help me to look to You right now. You are the author and perfecter of my faith. You are wise. You are gracious and merciful. You are the Prince of Peace.

As I stop to fix my eyes on You, to think on You and Your goodness and mercy, I can already feel my life beginning to center and calm. Even if there are storms all around me, I pray that You would give me the faith to rest and sleep—and even walk on water if You call me to come to You. Thank You that You calm the storms in my life. Thank You for Your promise and gift of peace.

I receive that with gratitude and in Your Son's name, right now.

Therefore, I urge you, brothers and sisters, in view of God's mercy, to offer your bodies as a living sacrifice, holy and pleasing to God—this is your true and proper worship. Do not conform to the pattern of this world, but be transformed by the renewing of your mind. Then you will be able to test and approve what God's will is—his good, pleasing, and perfect will.

—Romans 12:1–2 niv

Finally, brothers and sisters, whatever is true, whatever is noble, whatever is right, whatever is pure, whatever is lovely, whatever is admirable—if anything is excellent or praiseworthy—think about such things.

—Philippians 4:8 niv

The remarkable thing is, we have a choice every day regarding the attitude we will embrace for that day.

—Chuck Swindoll

I Need a New Attitude

God of Peace,

I do not feel at peace inside my heart and mind right now. I am struggling with an attitude that is muddying how I look at situations and even people I care about very much. I feel negative because something negative is inside me. I can pretend with some people that everything is okay, but You know my heart. And You know how it got that way.

I need You to give me a new outlook, based on a new heart inside of me. If I have unconfessed sin, a long-held resentment or grudge, a stubborn spirit, a fear, a refusal to forgive others, or some other act of disobedience that is nurturing this attitude, I pray You would help me receive Your grace at the source of the problem.

In faith and obedience, I give myself completely to You right now—including all my attitudes. I pray that You will renew my mind and heart so that I can see the world with fresh eyes, free from the snare of rotten attitudes.

In Jesus' name I pray this.

But blessed is the one who trusts in the Lord, whose confidence is in him. They will be like a tree planted by the water that sends out its roots by the stream. It does not fear when heat comes; its leaves are always green. It has no worries in a year of drought and never fails to bear fruit.

—JEREMIAH 17:7 NIV

I have strength for all things in Christ Who empowers me [I am ready for anything and equal to anything through Him Who infuses inner strength into me; I am self-sufficient in Christ's sufficiency].

—PHILIPPIANS 4:13 AMP

A humble person is more likely to be self-confident . . . a person with real humility knows how much they are loved.

—CORNELIUS PLANTINGA

I NEED CONFIDENCE

All Sufficient God,

You did not create me to live with a spirit of fear and timidity. I am more than a conqueror through Jesus Christ. I have every gift needed to make a difference in my world on behalf of You. No weapon formed against me—physical or emotional or spiritual—can defeat me.

But I confess I still live with a spirit of fear. I pray that through faith I would appropriate into my life all the riches You have given me. If there are events or repeated messages from my past that have blocked me from receiving what You have already given me, I hand all that to You now and ask that You deliver me from any such negativity.

You have come to give us abundant life. I don't want to miss out on that promise and provision because I lack confidence. Even if my emotions haven't caught up with my mind, I claim the confidence that is mine through Your blessed Son, Jesus Christ, right now. I will no longer back down from opportunities to serve and to have fellowship. I will not let fear rule my life. When I am tempted to lose my confidence, I will again proclaim Your promise that I can do all things through Christ who strengthens me.

In the mighty name of Jesus.

"In your anger do not sin": Do not let the sun go down while you are still angry, and do not give the devil a foothold.

—EPHESIANS 4:26–27 NIV

My dear brothers and sisters, take note of this: Everyone should be quick to listen, slow to speak and slow to become angry, because human anger does not produce the righteousness that God desires. Therefore, get rid of all moral filth and the evil that is so prevalent and humbly accept the word planted in you, which can save you.

—JAMES 1:19–21 NIV

Be ye angry, and sin not; therefore all anger is not sinful, because some degree of it, and on some occasions, is inevitable. But it becomes sinful and contradicts the rule of Scripture when it is conceived upon slight and inadequate provocation, and when it continues long.

—WILLIAM PALEY

I Am Struggling with Anger

Righteous God,

I know there is a good and holy anger. I know there are times when You want us to be angry at the things that make You angry. But I confess that I am struggling with a negative kind of anger.

It seems that everything makes me angry these days. I'm impatient. My temper is quick and ugly. I tell myself that I will control my temper but it still springs forth at the wrong time and in the wrong way.

I have tried to work on my anger with my own power and I have failed miserably. It is affecting me and those I love who are around me. I need a change.

God, I know You are able to do in me what I cannot do myself. I ask for Your help and healing. First of all, would You help me understand my temperament so I don't focus on changing how You have created me. But then I pray You will add to my life—my attitudes, my actions, my thoughts, my words—self-control and grace.

God, if there is unconfessed sin, lack of forgiveness offered or received, or anything else that is fostering my anger, I pray that You will help me deal with the root cause.

Thank You for Your help that I receive with gratitude, in Jesus' name.

Behold, I am with you and will keep you wherever you go, and will bring you back to this land; for I will not leave you until I have done what I have spoken to you.

—GENESIS 28:15 NKJV

And surely I am with you always, to the very end of the age.

—MATTHEW 28:20 NIV

Loneliness is the first thing which God's eye named, not good.

—JOHN MILTON

I Feel So Alone

My Father and My Friend,

You do not want us to feel alone and unwanted, but right now that's exactly how I feel. You created us to love one another, to be connected to one another, to serve and be served by one another. I feel cut off from friends and family.

If this loneliness I am feeling is a solitude You have put inside me for a season because You want me to draw closer to You, then I ask You to help me experience it with grace and gratitude. If it is because I am not treating others right and driving them off, I pray that You would help me make an immediate U-turn in how I interact with others. If it is because I am sending out unspoken messages that I want to be left alone, I ask that You help me make the first move in connecting with others. If it is because my social network is weak and filled with unkind and uncaring people, I pray that You help me find new settings for fellowship.

I thank You for hearing my cry of loneliness and helping me. I thank You most of all that You are always with me and will never forsake me.

In Jesus' kind name.

But He was wounded for our transgressions, He was bruised for our iniquities; the chastisement for our peace was upon Him, and by His stripes we are healed.

—ISAIAH 53:5 NKJV

This is the confidence we have in approaching God: that if we ask anything according to his will, he hears us.

—1 JOHN 5:14 NIV

Healing rain is a real touch from God. It could be physical healing or emotional or whatever.

—MICHAEL W. SMITH

I Need Healing

God of Mercy,

It is good to live in a time and place where advanced medical practice and innovation can treat so many illnesses and injuries. Our doctors are so good that we sometimes forget to rely on You, to turn to You as our Great Physician.

You know the medical condition I am facing right now. The doctors don't have a good prognosis and don't have answers.

I come to You in desperation and need. I need a miracle. I know that through the suffering of Jesus we receive salvation, but all works of grace come from His sacrifice, including healing—by His stripes we are healed.

In the name of Jesus, with all the faith within me—and it feels like the size of a mustard seed right now—I ask that You heal me. You bring sight to the blind, You make the lame to walk, and You can bring healing to me.

I pray that in this time of intense need and crisis I will learn lessons of faith, dependence, trust, and praise in all circumstances.

In Jesus' name.

Hear my cry, O God; attend to my prayer. From the
end of the earth I will cry to You, when my heart
is overwhelmed; lead me to the rock that is higher
than I. For You have been a shelter for me, a strong
tower from the enemy. I will abide in Your tabernacle
forever; I will trust in the shelter of Your wings.

—Psalm 61:1–4 nkjv

Your castles and strongholds shall have bars
of iron and bronze, and as your day, so shall
your strength, your rest and security, be.

—Deuteronomy 33:25 amp

Do not pray for easy lives. Pray to be stronger men.
Do not pray for tasks equal to your powers. Pray for
powers equal to your tasks. Then the doing of your work
shall be no miracle, but you shall be the miracle.

—Phillips Brooks

I Feel Overwhelmed

God of Strength,

I am not handling all that I am facing very well at the moment. I feel there is too much to be done and too little of me to do it. I am falling behind. I feel like an excessive burden is always on my shoulders. There is so much to be done that I'm not accomplishing much of anything.

First of all, I pray that You help me look at my life realistically and remove some unimportant tasks. Help me to simplify appropriately. Second, I pray that You would give me a spirit that is willing to accept challenges and work hard to meet them. If my work ethic is not where it should be, I ask for my determination and resolve. If I get in trouble because I procrastinate help me to get busy now. Third, I pray You will bring people into my life that will help me shoulder the load. Fourth, I pray You will strengthen me in every area of my life so that the tasks before me don't feel so heavy and simply aren't as hard.

But most of all I pray that You would be my helper. I pray that in every task I would be aware of Your presence. Help me understand that You will not allow more to come into my life than I can handle.

I pray this in the strong name of Jesus.

*Enter into His gates with thanksgiving and a thank offering
and into His courts with praise! Be thankful and say so to
Him, bless and affectionately praise His name! For the Lord
is good; His mercy and loving-kindness are everlasting,
His faithfulness and truth endure to all generations.*
—**Psalm 100:4–5 amp**

*Rejoice always, pray continually, give thanks in all
circumstances; for this is God's will for you in Christ Jesus.*
—**1 Thessalonians 5:16–18 niv**

*To be grateful is to recognize the love of God in everything
He has given us—and He has given us everything.
Every breath we draw is a gift of His love, every
moment of existence is a grace, for it brings
with it immense graces from Him.*
—**Thomas Merton**

Give Me a Thankful Heart

Dear Provider God,

I confess my sin of ingratitude. I have spent more time thinking about what I don't have than what I do have. I haven't appreciated the many gifts You have put into my life. I have taken friends and family members for granted. I don't want to live life negatively, with a sense of poverty—when You have made me rich with blessings.

Even as I say thank You right now for all the things You have done for and given to me, I pray that You enlarge my sense of gratitude and wonder. Make me the kind of person that blesses others because I recognize what they mean to me and tell them so.

Don't let me waste any more time with feelings of greed and jealousy. I want to experience each day as a gift to be savored and cherished.

Even if I have failed to say it at times, I am grateful to You, my God, who provides for my every need.

In the blessed name of Jesus I pray.

*"Therefore I tell you, do not worry about your life, what
you will eat or drink; or about your body, what you will
wear. Is not life more than food, and the body more than
clothes? Look at the birds of the air; they do not sow or reap
or store away in barns, and yet your heavenly Father feeds
them. Are you not much more valuable than they? Can any
one of you by worrying add a single hour to your life?"*

—MATTHEW 6:25–27 NIV

*For God did not give us a spirit of timidity (of cowardice,
of craven and cringing and fawning fear), but [He has
given us a spirit] of power and of love and of calm
and well-balanced mind and discipline and self-control.*

—2 TIMOTHY 1:7 AMP

*Worry does not empty tomorrow of its
sorrow; it empties today of its strength.*

—CORRIE TEN BOOM

I Am Worried

Faithful Heavenly Father,

I know in my head that I can trust You. That ultimately, all things work out wonderfully for those who love and trust You. I know that my life is in Your hands. But I am still living in a state of worry. I am afraid of what will happen tomorrow. I feel so much uncertainty in the world and in my life.

Jesus reminded us that flowers of the field are clothed and the birds of the air are fed—and that You care for me in much greater measure than these things. I pray that You would remind me now and throughout my day that You care for me. You care for me more than I care for myself. You love me to the extent that You gave Your very life for me.

I receive the assurance of Your presence right now. Even if fear and worry try to rob me of the joy of today, I will walk in confidence, knowing that You will be with me every step of the way. Even if my future plans are less than perfect, You will direct my steps.

Thank You for a peace that passes all understanding and that is greater than any sense of worry I feel.

In Jesus' matchless name.

Two are better than one, because they have a good reward for their labor. For if they fall, one will lift up his companion. But woe to him who is alone when he falls.

—ECCLESIASTES 4:10 NKJV

My command is this: Love each other as I have loved you. Greater love has no one than this: to lay down one's life for one's friends.

—JOHN 15:12–13 NIV

Friendship is born at that moment when one person says to another, "What! You too? I thought I was the only one."

—C.S. LEWIS

I Need a Friend

My Father and My Friend,

You alone can be counted on to be there for me in every moment and situation of life. But You have created us for friendship. Right now I don't feel connected and close to anyone. I feel like I am missing something important in life.

If I am doing something to keep others at a distance, I pray You would make me aware of how I can change and grow. I pray You will bring people into my life that I enjoy and can share mutual support with. I ask You to help me to reach out to others. If I am hanging out in the wrong places to make great friends, I pray that You will lead me to the right places, including the fellowship of church.

As humans we really do need each other. You have created us to support one another, to help each other with burdens and hurts. We are to share concern, kindness, and presence to make each other's life better.

I pray that I will always be the kind of person a friend can turn to for support. I pray I will find that kind of person for my life.

In Jesus' name.

In my distress [when seemingly closed in] I called upon
the Lord and cried to my God; He heard my voice
out of His temple (heavenly dwelling place),
and my cry came before Him, into His [very] ears.

—PSALM 18:6 AMP

My soul clings to the dust; revive me according to Your word.
I have declared my ways, and You answered me; teach me
Your statutes. Make me understand the way of Your precepts;
so shall I meditate on Your wonderful works. My soul melts
from heaviness; strengthen me according to Your word.

—PSALM 119:25–28 NKJV

It is important for us to make a distinction between the
spiritual fruit of joy and the cultural concept of happiness.
A Christian can have joy in his heart while there is still
spiritual depression in his head. The joy that we have
sustains us through these dark nights and is not
quenched by spiritual depression. The joy of the
Christian is one that survives all downturns in life.

—R. C. SPROUL

I Am Discouraged and Depressed

God of Comfort,

I come to You today with a sense of despair. I am so down I don't know if I'm discouraged or depressed, I just know there is a profound sorrow and heaviness in my heart. My strength and will seemed to be completely sapped. I can hardly move. I have pulled away from the people I love and need.

Even if others don't understand what I am going through right now—even if I don't understand it myself—thank You that You know exactly what I am going through. Your sorrow was so great that even the sweat of Your brow was droplets of blood. You know the dark night of the soul. You know what it is to experience anguish.

Thank You that You aren't judging me, but loving me. Knowing that You have walked through the valley of the shadow of death and will walk it again at my side is sweet comfort. It gives me the glimmer of hope I need, even if it does feel faint and fleeting right now.

I ask You for a special touch in my heart right now. I pray there will be awakening of hope and joy in spirit. I pray that You will make me more than an overcomer in this darkness I feel.

I love You because You first loved me. I will follow You.

In Jesus' merciful name.

*"Do not judge, and you will not be judged. Do
not condemn, and you will not be condemned.
Forgive, and you will be forgiven."*

—LUKE 6:37 NIV

*Therefore if you have any encouragement from being united
with Christ, if any comfort from his love, if any common
sharing in the Spirit, if any tenderness and compassion,
then make my joy complete by being like-minded,
having the same love, being one in spirit and of one mind.
Do nothing out of selfish ambition or vain conceit. Rather,
in humility value others above yourselves, not looking to your
own interests but each of you to the interests of the others.*

—PHILIPPIANS 2:1–4 NIV

*We should train ourselves, therefore, to see the good,
not the evil in others. We should speak approving words
of what is beautiful in them; not bitter, condemning words
of what may be imperfect or unlovely. We should look
at others through eyes of love, not through eyes of envy
or of selfishness. We should seek to heal with true affection's
gentleness, the things which are not as they should be.*

—J. R. MILLER

I Am Judgmental toward Others

Dear Lord,

I have fallen into an ugly and persistent pattern of judging others. I tend to see the evil, not the good; I notice what they do wrong, not what they do right; I interpret their words and deeds in a negative light. I fear my spirit of judgmentalism is worse than any deed I am judging!

I know we are called to be wise so that we can discern good from evil. But You have taught us that Your Spirit judges the heart of others and that our job is to love them, not to focus on fault-finding and criticizing.

The next time I start to judge harshly, even if it's only an unspoken thought, I ask You to put a check in my spirit. Remind me to seek Your forgiveness and move on positively. Most of all remind me that all of us have sinned and fallen short of Your glory—all of us are brought into Your presence by grace, by Your mercy and forgiveness.

I will not turn my eyes from wrongdoing, but enable me to see others with the love that You see them with. When I'm tempted to judge, help me to pray for that person instead.

Thank You that are making me more like You as I see and treat others like You do.

In Jesus' name.

WORK
AND
FINANCES

I have seen many men work without praying, though

I have never seen any good come out of it; but I

have never seen a man pray without working.

—HUDSON TAYLOR

And let the beauty and delightfulness and favor
of the Lord our God be upon us; confirm and establish
the work of our hands—yes, the work
of our hands, confirm and establish it.
—Psalm 90:17 amp

Let us not become weary in doing good, for at the proper
time we will reap a harvest if we do not give up.
—Galatians 6:9 niv

God give me work, till my life shall end
and life, till my work is done.
—Winifred Holtby

I Need a Job

Heavenly Father,

I am willing and ready to work. It is harder for me not to work than to work. Yes, there are some jobs I have turned down because they cannot support the financial obligations I am currently under. However if there is a lesser job than what I have had in the past that I need to accept for the purpose of humility and because there will be greater opportunities there, I pray that You help me to find pride in whatever I put my hand to.

I do ask that You would help me find the job that matches my abilities and training, that will meet my financial obligations, that will give me an opportunity to shine. I pray that my name would come to mind with friends and former colleagues who know of job opportunities that are right for me.

I pray that You would open doors for me as I seek interviews. Give me special creativity in finding the right employment situation. I ask for determination to keep turning my application in—even if I must face many rejections before finding the right job.

If there are special areas of service I can perform during this time of unemployment, I thank You for putting me to good use. I know there will be blessings within the tasks I perform—and perhaps service will be the avenue through which I find my next job.

I trust You to meet all my needs and I thank You that You are working on my behalf to find the right job.

In Jesus' mighty name.

But as for me, I watch in hope for the Lord,
I wait for God my Savior; my God will hear me.
—MICAH 7:7 NIV

And my God will meet all your needs according to
the riches of his glory in Christ Jesus. To our God
and Father be glory for ever and ever. Amen.
—PHILIPPIANS 4:19–20 NIV

Faith isn't the ability to believe long and far
into the misty future. It's simply taking God
at His Word and taking the next step.
—JONI EARECKSON TADA

I Have an Urgent Financial Need

Dear Lord,

I thought I was doing okay financially, but I have been hit hard by several surprises at once and I can't handle all the bills in front of me. I feel both numb and overwhelmed. This is very discouraging. I don't have any quick-fix solution in mind and don't know what to do next.

I do pray that You would bless me with a peace that can only come through You. I pray that I would be able to overcome any negative emotions to deal with this with a clear mind. I pray for wisdom and creativity to handle this. I pray for mercy from those I owe money—and for the poise and courage to speak to them directly.

You own the earth and everything on it, so I ask that You would send a miracle to provide relief in this situation. I pray that even though the urgent need in front of me came as a surprise, You already knew this was coming and were not taken off-guard, for nothing is hidden from You.

I know You will deliver me, O Lord, and I thank You in advance for meeting my every need. I pray for a blessing and an improvement in my overall finances.

In Jesus' name.

Blessed is the one who perseveres under trial because,
having stood the test, that person will receive the crown
of life that the Lord has promised to those who love him.
—James 1:12 niv

Whatever you do, work at it with all your heart,
as working for the Lord, not for human masters, since you
know that you will receive an inheritance from
the Lord as a reward. It is the Lord Christ you are serving.
—Colossians 3:23–24 niv

Comfort and prosperity have never enriched
the world as much as adversity has.
—Billy Graham

My Company Is Struggling

Wise Father,

I feel like I am doing great work and doing all I can to help my company, but our business is simply not in good shape. Revenue and profits are down. Customers aren't happy. Morale inside the company is poor. There is open conflict. Even the top leaders seem to be at a loss as to what to do. I am fearful that I will end up being out of a job.

God, help me to be faithful in my efforts; help me to build morale up, not tear it down; help me to offer constructive ideas in a positive manner.

If there is nothing I can do to help and this is a time for me to make a change in where I work, help me to do so carefully and with grace. If You have lessons to teach me by fighting through this time of adversity, I pray I will give it my best shot. And I pray that others will join me so that we dramatically change our company's circumstances. I pray that our product and services will meet the needs of our customers—and that we will gain new customers until our financial situation is turned around.

Even though I work for a company, I ultimately work for You, O God. I will always give You my best effort.

In Jesus' name.

*There is nothing better for a man than that he should
eat and drink and make himself enjoy good in his labor.
Even this, I have seen, is from the hand of God.
For to the person who pleases Him God gives wisdom and
knowledge and joy; but to the sinner He gives the work
of gathering and heaping up, that he may give
to one who pleases God. This also is vanity
and a striving after the wind and a feeding on it.*

—ECCLESIASTES 2:24,26 AMP

*Do your best to present yourself to God as one
approved, a worker who does not need to be ashamed
and who correctly handles the word of truth.*

—2 TIMOTHY 2:15 NIV

*Those times when you feel like quitting can be times of great
opportunity, for God uses your troubles to help you grow.*

—WARREN WIERSBE

I Am Unhappy in My Work

Heavenly Father,

I know that not every aspect of work—or anything else in life—can be pleasant and fun. I know there are times when hard effort is required. I also know that work is honorable and important and necessary for supporting my family and myself. But I am in a work situation that I dislike very much. I find no internal reward or fulfillment based on what I am doing.

Father, if there is something in my attitude that needs correcting and I'm completely at fault in these feelings, I lay my life before You and ask You to place in me a new heart and a new way of looking at this work. If You want me to stay in this job for a season—or if there simply aren't any other viable options—I pray that I will perform tasks and get along with fellow workers to the best of my ability. I pray that I would make my job a better situation through my attitude and actions. I pray that I would be positive and diligent and reveal my character and my honor for You.

If this unhappiness is a sign I need to look for new employment, I pray that I would still leave here on the best of terms. I pray that You will bring new opportunities across my path. I pray for Your guidance for every step that goes into that decision.

In the name of my Savior.

*Therefore if you bring your gift to the altar, and there
remember that your brother has something against you,
leave your gift there before the altar, and go your way. First be
reconciled to your brother, and then come and offer your gift.*

—Matthew 5:23–24 nkjv

*He has shown you, O mortal, what is good.
And what does the Lord require of you? To act justly
and to love mercy and to walk humbly with your God.*

—Micah 6:8 niv

*I have always found that mercy bears
richer fruits than strict justice.*

—Abraham Lincoln

I Am Being Sued

God of Righteousness,

I have to appear in a court of law because I have been sued. I don't believe the suit has merit or that I have wronged anyone, but I am still fearful because it is so hard to predict the legal system.

I need Your courage, wisdom, and protection. If I have in fact legitimately harmed someone, I ask that You would reveal a clear and mutually acceptable settlement.

If this goes to court, I pray that my legal defense would carefully and thoroughly address all pertinent points of law and that the suit would be struck down.

I pray that my finances and most of all my reputation would not be damaged through this process. Please calm my spirit during the waiting period.

I pray that I would be respectful of my judge and the legal system. I pray that I would be poised throughout this process and would not submit to the temptation to become angry, spiteful, and vengeful toward my adversary.

I ask again that this case be settled in my favor.

In Jesus' holy name.

*Wait and hope for and expect the Lord; be brave
and of good courage and let your heart be stout and
enduring. Yes, wait for and hope for and expect the Lord.*

—**Psalm 27:14 amp**

*You who are servants, be good servants to your masters—
not just to good masters, but also to bad ones. What counts
is that you put up with it for God's sake when you're treated
badly for no good reason. There's no particular virtue in
accepting punishment that you well deserve. But if you're
treated badly for good behavior and continue in spite of
it to be a good servant, that is what counts with God.*

—**1 Peter 2:18–20 The Message**

*We can't control difficult people and we can't change
them, but with God's guidance we can understand
them better and find a way to cope with them.*

—**Jake Zavada**

I Need Favor with My Boss

Good and Gracious God,

I have a difficult boss. I don't know why they don't seem to like me or my work, but they are making that very obvious. I feel like I am giving good effort and doing my job correctly. I feel like I am respectful to customers and clients, colleagues, and my boss. I need your help in this situation.

First, help me to evaluate myself honestly to confirm that I am dong the job with a good attitude and good results. Second, would You search my heart for disrespect and anger toward authorities in general, and this boss in particular? If there is a grievance in my heart that is showing up in ways I am not even aware of, I pray that You would begin a work to make my heart new.

If working for this boss isn't going to change for the foreseeable future, help me to use this time wisely to grow in my self-confidence and learn the important work and life lesson of acting with poise under fire and adversity. I pray that this will not hold me back in my work and career but help me to move forward and grow. I know that You are able to take negative situations and turn them into something positive on my behalf.

When I submit to my boss, I am doing it out of submission to You, Lord.

In Jesus' name.

For not from the east nor from the west nor from the
south come promotion and lifting up. But God is the
Judge! He puts down one and lifts up another.

—PSALM 75:6–7 AMP

Humble yourselves in the sight
of the Lord, and He will lift you up.

—JAMES 4:10 NKJV

Your attitude, not your aptitude,
will determine your altitude.

—ZIG ZIGLAR

I Want a Job Promotion

Heavenly Father,

Thank You that You invite me to bring what is on my heart before You. I would like to be promoted at work. I believe I am willing and ready for advancement. I pray this with all confidence and trust knowing that ultimately it is You who will promote me in life.

I do pray that You will bring my name before those in my organization who are responsible for promotion. I know that I need to continue to grow in skills to better be able to lead others. If there are any ways that I am hurting my chance for promotion, I pray You would bring them to my attention so I can work to improve those areas.

If part of getting promoted is me positively bringing it up to my boss, I pray that You would give me the right words and the right time to do so.

If You have a better opportunity for me that doesn't include a promotion at this moment, I pray that You will reveal Your plans for me in my heart and mind. I am open to any better plans You have for my life!

I affirm that promotion ultimately comes from You and I will not forget to thank and praise You for Your work on my behalf. Thank You, Father, for being my hope and help.

In Jesus' name.

Hezekiah trusted in the Lord, the God of Israel. . . . He held
fast to the Lord and did not stop following him; he kept the
commands the Lord had given Moses. And the Lord was
with him; he was successful in whatever he undertook.

—2 KINGS 18:5–7 NIV

But even if you should suffer for what is right, you are blessed.
"Do not fear their threats; do not be frightened."
But in your hearts revere Christ as Lord. Always be
prepared to give an answer to everyone who asks you to
give the reason for the hope that you have. But do this with
gentleness and respect, keeping a clear conscience, so that
those who speak maliciously against your good behavior in
Christ may be ashamed of their slander. For it is better, if it
is God's will, to suffer for doing good than for doing evil.

—1 PETER 3:14–17 NIV

Spiritual growth depends on two things: first, a willingness
to live according to the Word of God; second, a willingness
to take whatever consequences emerge as a result.

—SINCLAIR B. FERGUSON

I Am Being Asked to Compromise My Character

God of Righteousness,

You know I want to be a person of honor. I don't want to jeopardize my character and reputation for a temporary and dishonest benefit. You know every detail of my situation at work and how I am being asked to compromise on my principles. You know that I am tempted to surrender my principles in order to not make others unhappy and because it would be easier.

If I am misjudging what is being asked of me, I pray that You would make that clear and obvious to me. I don't want to falsely accuse anyone I work with of unethical practices. But I know that You have called me to love righteousness, to be fair and honest in all my dealings, and that is exactly what I need Your help to do.

God, help me to be courageous to stand up for what is right. Help me to clearly communicate my objections to unethical behavior. Help me to be redemptive in this situation, so that my company and my colleagues know there is a better way of doing business that will be of greater benefit and reward in the long run. And God, I ask that You protect me from anyone who would seek to damage me and my position for taking a stand.

You saved Daniel from the lion's den and I know You will save me. Thank You, in Jesus' name.

*The Lord will open to you His good treasure, the heavens,
to give the rain to your land in its season, and to bless all the
work of your hand. You shall lend to many nations, but you
shall not borrow. And the Lord will make you the head and
not the tail; you shall be above only, and not be beneath, if
you heed the commandments of the Lord your God, which
I command you today, and are careful to observe them.*

—DEUTERONOMY 28:12–13 NKJV

*Each of you should give what you have decided
in your heart to give, not reluctantly or under compulsion,
for God loves a cheerful giver. And God is able to bless
you abundantly, so that in all things at all times, having
all that you need, you will abound in every good work.*

—2 CORINTHIANS 2:7–8 NIV

*Gratitude is an offering precious in the sight of God,
and it is one that the poorest of us can make and
be not poorer but richer for having made it.*

—A. W. TOZER

I Want to Be a Cheerful Giver

Dear God of All Generosity,

I can never thank You enough for everything You have given to me. You created a wonderful world for me to live in. You gave me the breath of life. You have redeemed me when I was a a slave in my sins. You have brought countless blessings into my life.

I want to be like You. I want to be like Jesus. I want to be a cheerful giver. But I confess that I struggle to be generous. Sometimes I don't plan well and I'm simply short on extra funds. Sometimes I follow habits and keep spending on myself with little thought for others. I buy things I don't need and lose interest shortly after I possess them. I sometimes worry I won't have enough for myself and hold tightly to what I have. I forget that You are the giver of all good gifts.

God I pray You will give me a heart like Yours. Help me to see those around me like You do. Give me a love in my heart that sees giving as the joyful act of worship that it is, not as something that is a painful sacrifice. I pray that my generosity would include giving from my finances, but spill over into all forms of kindness and service. Help me to open my eyes to the opportunities to experience joy through giving to those in need.

In Jesus' blessed name.

This day I call the heavens and the earth as witnesses against you that I have set before you life and death, blessings and curses. Now choose life, so that you and your children may live and that you may love the LORD your God, listen to his voice, and hold fast to him. For the LORD is your life, and he will give you many years in the land he swore to give to your fathers, Abraham, Isaac, and Jacob.

—**DEUTERONOMY 30:19–20** NIV

The soul of a lazy man desires, and has nothing; but the soul of the diligent shall be made rich.

—**PROVERBS 13:4** NKJV

Procrastination is like a credit card: it's a lot of fun until you get the bill.

—**CHRISTOPHER PARKER**

I Need to Get Things Done

Dear God,

I am having a terrible struggle with procrastination. I can't seem to focus on the task at hand. I get distracted. I take a break. I shuffle around my to-do list. I keep moving things that need to be done today into the future. Then I have to deal with multiple and competing priorities in a crisis mode. It is affecting not only my work, but also my relationships and sense of self-esteem.

I want to change, God. I know that I need to stop procrastinating. I know I need to tackle my tasks with enthusiasm and in a timely and well-ordered fashion. I haven't been able to make myself do what I need to do.

I ask that You would help me to do what I can't do in my own strength. I pray that this moment of prayer would be the start of a change in my attitudes and behaviors when it comes to work. I pray that I would enjoy the benefits and blessings of productivity today and gain momentum toward a new way of doing things.

You tell us to not grumble and complain about life and work. I ask You to forgive me for my attitudes and choices that have created this situation. I pray for strength and wisdom to dig myself out of this rut and onto a new level path of living. I am thankful for the opportunity to work and serve to make a living—and to bring honor to Your name. I work for You today.

In Jesus' mighty name.

*Very truly I tell you, my Father will give you
whatever you ask in my name. Until now you have
not asked for anything in my name. Ask and you
will receive, and your joy will be complete.*

—JOHN 16:23–24 NIV

*"Ask and it will be given to you; seek and you will find; knock
and the door will be opened to you. For everyone who asks
receives; the one who seeks finds; and to the one who knocks,
the door will be opened. Which of you, if your son asks for
bread, will give him a stone? Or if he asks for a fish, will give
him a snake? If you, then, though you are evil, know how to
give good gifts to your children, how much more will your
Father in heaven give good gifts to those who ask him!"*

—MATTHEW 7:7–11 NIV

*If therefore our houses be houses of the Lord, we shall for
that reason love home, reckoning our daily devotion the
sweetest of our daily delights; and our family-worship
the most valuable of our family-comforts. . . . A church
in the house will be a good legacy, nay, it will be a good
inheritance, to be left to your children after you.*

—MATTHEW HENRY

I Would Like a New Home

Heavenly Father,

I have everything I need in life. I am so blessed. I do come to You today with a special request. I would like a new home. You know the specific reasons (size, neighborhood, number of bedrooms) that have put this on my mind.

I know there are many people in the world that do not have a roof over their head. There are homeless and displaced people in this country and especially around the world. I am truly grateful for the home I have right now. But You invite me to bring my needs and even my wants and desires to You, so I do so at this time. I know You will let me know if You think I should stay where I am at and I thank You for Your guidance in all my life.

Thank You for Your love and countless blessings. If it is Your will, I pray that You will help me to find the perfect new home that meets my family's needs. I pray that it will be in the price range that I can afford and that I will be able to secure financing. I pray that any move would go smoothly and with no accidents.

Even as I pray for a new home, I pray that I would make whatever home I live in a place of worship and hospitality in Your name.

I pray this in Jesus' name.

"For I know the plans I have for you,"
says the Lord. "They are plans for good and not
for disaster, to give you a future and a hope."
—JEREMIAH 29:11 NLT

He will still be with you to teach you. You will see your
teacher with your own eyes. Your own ears will hear
him. Right behind you a voice will say, "This is the way
you should go," whether to the right or to the left.
—ISAIAH 30:20-21 NLT

It is amazing how many people let life happen to them rather
than asking God for wisdom in their decisions. He promises
to give you wisdom and knowledge for everything you do.
When you make a decision knowing that it is based on the
wisdom of God, joy and peace cannot help but follow.
—DON CLOWERS

I Have a Big Opportunity

Wise and Gracious Father,

I thank You for the many ways You have led and directed me in my life. I am thankful for where I am in life because I know You have brought me here. I already have all the riches of Your grace and that's all that really matters. But now I have a new opportunity in front of me. It requires a lot of change and will affect the people closest to me.

I want to grow and be all that You want me to be. But that doesn't mean every open door is the right door for me to walk through. I need You to speak to me now with Your wisdom and direction. Even more importantly, I need You to help settle my mind and spirit so I can hear Your voice. Your pathways lead to peace, so I pray for a sense of Your peace, whether my answer needs to be yes or no.

Help me to think clearly through all the issues that this opportunity presents. I want to serve You and honor You in all my decisions. Since You have promised to order my steps, even if I don't feel a clear-cut impression from Your spirit, I will make this decision with confidence, knowing that You honor a faithful heart.

Knowing that many people are looking for an opportunity, I thank You that this decision is in front of me. It is a reminder that You meet all my needs.

I commit this opportunity to you in Jesus' name.

It is of the Lord's mercies that we are not consumed, because his compassions fail not. They are new every morning: great is thy faithfulness. The Lord is my portion, saith my soul; therefore will I hope in him.

—LAMENTATIONS 3:22–24 KJV

I waited patiently for the Lord; he turned to me and heard my cry. He lifted me out of the slimy pit, out of the mud and mire; he set my feet on a rock and gave me a firm place to stand.

—PSALM 40:1–2 NIV

Concentrate on counting your blessings and you'll have little time to count anything else.

—WOODROW KROLL

I Am Having Financial Difficulties

Dear Almighty God,

I can't believe my finances are in such bad shape. I feel buried in debt. I feel like my future is mortgaged. I feel stress just trying to keep payments current. I don't see any practical way to get out of the money troubles I find myself in.

O God, You are the giver of all good gifts. You own everything in the earth. You know and meet all our needs. I come to You in prayer, asking for Your divine touch. I am asking You to help me in ways I can't see for myself.

I do ask that You forgive me for wrong attitudes and practices I have in regard to finances. Greed. Overspending. Lack of discipline. Lack of planning. I pray that You will transform the things I have done wrong and turn them into strengths that come from inside of me.

I ask You to give me the strength and courage to look at my situation honestly; to seek out wise counsel; to make realistic plans; to communicate and negotiate clearly and fairly with creditors.

I pray that You will open my eyes to see opportunities to increase my income. I pray that new attitudes and practices will take hold in my life so that when I dig out of this mess—and I know You are helping me do just that—it will never happen again.

You are the God of peace and I ask for Your peace as this situation is turned around. In Jesus' name I pray this.

*He gives wisdom to the wise and knowledge to the
discerning. He reveals deep and hidden things; he knows
what lies in darkness, and light dwells with him.*

—**DANIEL 2:21–22 NIV**

*For in him all things were created: things in heaven
and on earth, visible and invisible, whether thrones
or powers or rulers or authorities; all things have
been created through him and for him. He is before
all things, and in him all things hold together.*

—**COLOSSIANS 1:16–17 NIV**

*We are ourselves creations. We are meant to continue
creativity by being creative ourselves. This is the God-
force extending itself through us. Creativity is God's
gift to us. Using creativity is our gift back to God.*

—**JULIA CAMERON**

I Need Creativity in My Life

Creator God,

You are the creator of the universe and all that is—and You have made us in Your image. So I know that You have created us to be creative—to see things that don't yet exist, to connect existing ideas to come up with something bold and new. But right now I don't feel very creative, God. I feel like my ideas are stale and that is making my work and relationships and conversations just as stale.

I ask that You would renew in me the sense of wonder that You gave me as a child. I pray that I would open my eyes to the beauty and intricacy of the world around me. I pray that I wouldn't just go through the motions but would really engage with people and listen and learn. I pray that I would open Your Word with fresh eyes and that I would read better books and watch better shows to stimulate my imagination.

Whatever You bring to my mind, I pray that I would honor You with it and give You the glory for being the giver of all good gifts.

I thank You that even now You are helping me to see the depths and riches of Your love for me and the wonders of Your world. Thank You for planting in me the spark of creativity and help me to create ideas that make a difference in my work, my relationships, and my world.

In the name of the One who was with You in creation!

The rich rule over the poor,

and the borrower is slave to the lender.

—PROVERBS 22:7 NIV

"Suppose one of you wants to build a tower. Won't you first

sit down and estimate the cost to see if you have enough

money to complete it? For if you lay the foundation and are

not able to finish it, everyone who sees it will ridicule you,

saying, 'This person began to build and wasn't able to finish.'"

—LUKE 14:28–30 NIV

When we surrender every area of our lives—

including our finances—to God, then we are free to

trust Him to meet our needs. But if we would rather

hold tightly to those things that we possess, then we

find ourselves in bondage to those very things.

—LARRY BURKETT

I Need to Live within My Means

God Who Provides,

More money is going out than is coming in every single month. It's not a huge difference, but my debt load is adding up. I've rationalized spending more than I make with thoughts that I will make more and spend less in the future. I'm not sure about more money, but the future is now in spending less money. But I need Your help.

I pray first of all for the honesty to look at my finances exactly as they are. I pray for wisdom to write down a plan on how I am going to spend my money. I pray for obedience so that I add the tithe to my budget—knowing that if I worship You with this then everything else seems to fall into place. I pray then for courage and determination to follow the plan. Even if the mountain of debt looks insurmountable I ask You to give me the determination to press forward with this plan.

You know my temptations and weaknesses when it comes to spending. If I need to stop eating out every day, I pray that I would have the common sense to pack a lunch. If there are sinful vices in my life, help me to cut those off immediately. Help me to eradicate whatever is keeping me from living within my means.

You are the provider of all that I need. I ask that You help me to live with the peace that comes from living within my means.

In Jesus' name.

SPIRITUAL GROWTH

Prayer—secret, fervent, believing prayer—

lies at the root of all personal godliness.

—WILLIAM CAREY

No temptation has overtaken you except what is common to mankind. And God is faithful; he will not let you be tempted beyond what you can bear. But when you are tempted, he will also provide a way out so that you can endure it.

—1 Corinthians 10:13 NIV

"Not by might nor by power, but by my Spirit," says the Lord Almighty.

—Zechariah 4:6 NIV

If we do not abide in prayer, we will abide in temptation. Let this be one aspect of our daily intercession: "God, preserve my soul, and keep my heart and all its ways so that I will not be entangled." When this is true in our lives, a passing temptation will not overcome us. We will remain free while others lie in bondage.

—John Owen

I Am Struggling with Temptation

Dear God,

I am losing the battle with temptation right now. You know I want to do the right thing. But I am consistently doing the opposite of what I know is right, of what You want and expect from me. I am disappointed and embarrassed in myself. I am discouraged that I am defeated so easily. Spiritual defeats have me barely hanging on to my faith.

Thank You first of all that You know the power of temptation and understand what I am going through. Thank You for offering instant forgiveness. You promised that if I confess my sin You are faithful to forgive that sin and all my sins. Thank You most of all that You still love me, even when I give in to temptation.

I confess I simply don't have the strength to win my spiritual battles. I can't do it. What I am specifically asking for now is a strength to overcome the temptations that I don't possess through good intentions and personal determination. My own efforts haven't worked. Please give me Your strength. Go before me. Fight my battles with me and for me. Do for me what I can't do myself. Thank You for turning my weakness into strength.

May you be strengthened with all power,
according to his glorious might, for all
endurance and patience with joy.

—COLOSSIANS 1:11 ESV

Let us lay aside every weight, and the sin
which so easily ensnares us, and let us run with
endurance the race that is set before us.

—HEBREWS 12:1 NKJV

That which is bitter to endure
may be sweet to remember.

—THOMAS FULLER

I Need Endurance

God of Strength,

I know a relationship with You is not like a hundred meter sprint; one quick burst and it's finished. But rather, You desire a relationship with me that is like a marathon, covering every day of my life. I confess that my endurance is lacking right now, God. I get distracted too easily. I get discouraged. I feel self-sufficient. I take things for granted and forget to be thankful—especially to You.

You know the unhealthy dynamics that I have allowed to accumulate in my life, slowing my pace and causing me to stumble. I ask that You would grant me the resolve and the grace to rid myself of habits and attitudes that keep me from fully serving and loving You. I pray that You give me an undefeatable spirit that learns to run long distances without grumbling, ready and willing to go as far and long as You ask of me. I know I can't just manufacture this mindset, so in faith I ask that You increase and develop what strength You have already given me.

Thank You, gracious Father, that You await me at the ultimate finish line of life with an embrace and crown that will last forever!

Confess to one another therefore your faults (your slips, your false steps, your offenses, your sins) and pray [also] for one another, that you may be healed and restored [to a spiritual tone of mind and heart]. The earnest (heartfelt, continued) prayer of a righteous man makes tremendous power available [dynamic in its working].

—JAMES 5:16 AMP

Devote yourselves to prayer, being watchful and thankful.

—COLOSSIANS 4:2 NIV

*Satan trembles when he sees
the weakest Christian on his knees.*

—WILLIAM COWPER

I Want to Be Strong in Prayer

Dear God,

What an incredible privilege, what an honor, what a personal blessing that You have invited me to come into Your very presence through prayer. Forgive me for the times when I have not been faithful to pray because I thought I was too busy. Forgive me for the times that I have lacked the faith to believe that prayer changes the world—and that prayer changes me.

God, I acknowledge that I need to pray for my own spiritual well-being and for the various needs in my life. I also know there are friends and family who need my prayers. There is a lost and hurting world that needs me to be a prayer warrior.

I recommit myself right now to being a person of prayer. I will pray alone and with others. I will pray morning, noon, and night. I will voice words to You and I will be silent to listen for Your voice. Thank You that more and more I will become the person You want me to be through Your gracious invitation to talk with You each day.

In the wonderful name of Jesus.

*So rend your heart, and not your garments; return to the
Lord your God, for He is gracious and merciful, slow to anger,
and of great kindness; and He relents from doing harm.*

—JOEL 2:13 NKJV

*We must pay more careful attention, therefore,
to what we have heard, so that we do not drift away.*

—HEBREWS 2:1 NIV

*A life without a purpose is a languid, drifting thing.
Every day we ought to renew our purpose, saying to
ourselves: This day let us make a sound beginning,
for what we have hitherto done is naught.*

—THOMAS À KEMPIS

I Have Drifted Spiritually and Need to Come "Home"

Gracious Heavenly Father,

I have experienced all the joys and blessings of being called Your child. But lately I have drifted away. I don't know why I have lost my commitment and enthusiasm for being a member of Your family and I don't know how it's happened, but I confess that I have drifted in my spiritual life. I have not paid attention to the state of my soul. I have not kept my eyes on You.

I know and believe that nothing is more important in life than my relationship with You. You are the one who turns darkness to light; who forgives me of sin and offers me a new life; who welcomes me with open arms, even after I've wondered far from home.

Right now I affirm my love for You. I come to You humbly. My faith feels weak but I bring You my praise and worship. I ask You to do a brand new work in my heart and life. Even if I don't feel an immediate emotional confirmation, I confidently affirm that You are rekindling the flame of faith inside of me. Like the Father did for the Prodigal Son, You forgive me, embrace me and include me in Your family.

"And when you stand praying, if you hold anything
against anyone, forgive them, so that your Father
in heaven may forgive you your sins."
—MARK 11:25 NIV

Therefore, as God's chosen people, holy and dearly loved,
clothe yourselves with compassion, kindness, humility,
gentleness and patience. Bear with each other and forgive
one another if any of you has a grievance against someone.
Forgive as the Lord forgave you. And over all these virtues
put on love, which binds them all together in perfect unity.
—COLOSSIANS 3:12–14 NIV

If someone has wronged you, and you get
revenge, you will be pleased for a minute. If you
forgive him, you will be happy forever.
—AUTHOR UNKNOWN

I Need to Forgive

Dear God of My Salvation,

You reached out to me in kindness before I ever gave You the time of day. You offered me forgiveness for my sins before I was even willing to admit to them. You loved me when my attitudes and actions made me very unlovable. Thank You for the way You treated me with compassion. Thank You for not giving up on me when I was too stubborn to change. Thank You for giving me the mercy I did not deserve.

Now I need to forgive someone else. And I admit I am struggling to do so. I know it is the right thing to do but I am struggling with the hurt and anger of what this person has done.

First, I thank You that You offer me the same opportunity to be compassionate, loving, and forgiving to others who are just as stubborn and deserving as I have been. In Your model prayer You teach us to ask for forgiveness even as we forgive others.

Let my act of forgiveness remind me of the incredible sacrifice of Jesus Christ so that I understand the power of forgiveness to change things—especially me. Even if the person I need to forgive isn't responsive, I pray that I'll be thankful in remembrance of what You have done for me!

In Jesus' precious name.

In everything set them an example by doing what is good. In your teaching show integrity, seriousness and soundness of speech that cannot be condemned, so that those who oppose you may be ashamed because they have nothing bad to say about us.

—TITUS 2:7–8 NIV

Let no one despise or think less of you because of your youth, but be an example (pattern) for the believers in speech, in conduct, in love, in faith, and in purity.

—1 TIMOTHY 4:12 AMP

I choose faithfulness. . . . Today I will keep my promises. My debtors will not regret their trust. My associates will not question my word. My wife will not question my love. And my children will never fear that their father will not come home.

—MAX LUCADO

I Want to Be an Example
of Faith and Integrity

Dear Lord,

You have called people who know You to be examples of faith, purity, and integrity. We show to the world the nature and power of the Gospel of Jesus Christ through the ways we live our lives.

Lord, I want to be a person who honors Your name because of the way I live. Please protect me from temptation and evil ways. Help me to never get caught in a lifestyle of sin that will damage the cause of the gospel in an unbeliever's eyes.

Instead, Lord, let me exhibit qualities of grace, godly passion and enthusiasm, joyfulness, gratitude, gentleness, wisdom, generosity, honesty, kindness, faithfulness, and all the other fruit of the Spirit that demonstrate to a skeptical world just how wonderful it is to know You. May my life be an example of Your power and grace.

In Jesus' gracious name.

And I will give you shepherds after my own heart, who

will feed you with knowledge and understanding.

—JEREMIAH 3:15 ESV

Command and teach these things. Don't let anyone look

down on you because you are young, but set an example

for the believers in speech, in conduct, in love, in faith

and in purity. Until I come, devote yourself to the public

reading of Scripture, to preaching and to teaching. Do not

neglect your gift, which was given you through prophecy

when the body of elders laid their hands on you.

—1 TIMOTHY 4:11–14 NIV

If sheep do not have the constant care of a shepherd, they

will go the wrong way, unaware of the dangers at hand.

They have been known to nibble themselves right off the

side of a mountain. . . . And so, because sheep are sheep,

they need shepherds to care for them. The welfare of sheep

depends solely upon the care they get from their shepherd.

Therefore, the better the shepherd, the healthier the sheep.

—KAY ARTHUR

Bless My Pastor

Good Shepherd,

I thank You for the pastor You have called to my church. Thank You for their kindness and faithfulness. Thank You for their teaching that is built on Your Word.

I pray a special blessing for my pastor today. They serve others in so many ways. They work with people going through incredibly tough situations. And not everyone they minister to is responsive to You or to their efforts. They see and know about problems that must discourage them sometimes.

I ask that they would feel Your presence in a special way today. Even as they encourage others, I pray You would bring encouragers across their path. I pray that I would be one of those who supports and loves my pastor even when I don't agree with every decision. I pray that as my pastor opens Your Word today to study what You would speak directly into their heart. Give them a message that blesses our congregation but that is also a blessing in their own life. Guard their heart from discouragement and temptation. Give them strength for every task. Give them a vision that will guide this church to growth and spiritual vitality.

In Jesus' name.

There has never been the slightest doubt in my mind that the God who started this great work in you would keep at it and bring it to a flourishing finish on the very day Christ Jesus appears.

—**PHILIPPIANS 1:6 THE MESSAGE**

Consider it pure joy, my brothers and sisters, whenever you face trials of many kinds, because you know that the testing of your faith produces perseverance. Let perseverance finish its work so that you may be mature and complete, not lacking anything.

—**JAMES 1:2–4 NIV**

Maturity doesn't come with age; it comes with acceptance of responsibility.

—**ED COLE**

I NEED TO MATURE

Heavenly Father,

Your desire for us is not that we are comfortable or happy all the time but that we continue to grow into mature and complete Christians. The process of becoming Christ-like lasts a lifetime. I feel like I'm not very far on that journey. I confess that I am tossed back and forth with the waves of my circumstances. I'm up and down emotionally and spiritually. I get frustrated and short-tempered and jealous and competitive with others too easily.

Just as salvation is a free gift of grace, I know that growth is also based on Your work on the cross. My job is to be willing and ready to submit to Your will in my life. I do that right now. I do say "yes" to anything You would ask of me. I open up every area of my life to You—my relationships, thought life, entertainment choices, attitudes, and conversations.

Thank You that You are faithful to not only forgive me for my sins, but to empower me to grow into the person You want me to be—mature, complete, lacking in nothing.

I receive Your grace with all faith and gratitude.

In Jesus' holy name.

The Lord is compassionate and gracious, slow to anger,
abounding in love. He will not always accuse, nor will
he harbor his anger forever; he does not treat us as
our sins deserve or repay us according to our iniquities.
For as high as the heavens are above the earth, so great
is his love for those who fear him; as far as the east is from
the west, so far has he removed our transgressions from us.

—**PSALM 103:8–12 NIV**

We all, like sheep, have gone astray, each of
us has turned to our own way; and the Lord
has laid on him the iniquity of us all.

—**ISAIAH 53:6 NIV**

What if thou hadst committed the sins of a thousand?
What if thou hadst committed the sins of a million
worlds? Christ's righteousness will cover, Christ's
blood will cleanse thee from the guilt of all.

—**GEORGE WHITEFIELD**

I Need to Be Forgiven

Gracious Lord,

I have received the gift of salvation that You offered me in Jesus Christ but I have strayed from my relationship with You. I have done wrong and sinned. And I am so sorry for that. I am embarrassed by my actions. I don't want to be the kind of person that is always up and down spiritually. I want to be able to walk faithfully.

Lord, I know it is not by good works that I am saved. It is a free gift from You. I know that when it comes to our spiritual life, humans are like sheep—all have wandered and fallen astray. Help me to live as You want me to, help me to trust more instead of trying harder. Help my conscience to always be sensitive and not be numbed by all the bad things in the world so that I will always seek You immediately for forgiveness if I do wrong.

I pray that I will be aware of Your presence through the Holy Spirit so I will avoid temptations and the sins that so easily entangle me.

Forgive me now. Cover my sins. Make my heart whiter than snow so that I will be blameless before You. As far as the east is from the west I pray that You will forgive and forget my sins.

I pray for and and receive Your forgiveness through the blood of Jesus.

Let us consider how we may spur one another

on toward love and good deeds.

—Hebrews 10:24 niv

May the God who gives endurance and encouragement

give you the same attitude of mind toward each other that

Christ Jesus had, so that with one mind and one voice you

may glorify the God and Father of our Lord Jesus Christ.

—Romans 15:5–6 niv

I know why I am here and my only real focused goal is to

live each day to the fullest and to try and honor God and

be an encouragement to others. What the future holds is

firmly in God's hands, and I am very happy about that!

—Ken Hensley

I Want to Encourage Others

Heavenly Father,

You have created us to affirm one another and to be a blessing to our families, communities, and the entire world. But it is so easy to become consumed with our own challenges and problems and forget that those around us are struggling too.

I think of my closest friends. Father, I ask that You would give me words of encouragement for each one of them. Help me find a way to lift them up and show them Your love in tangible ways. Help me to fan the flames of their faith in You. Help me to gently remind them that they were created by You for love and good deeds.

You alone empower us to accomplish Your will in the world, but I am humbled—and excited—to know that You can use even me to bring about Your plans. I am willing, Lord.

In Jesus' precious name.

For God is not a God of disorder but of peace.

—1 CORINTHIANS 14:33 NLT

Trust in the Lord with all your heart, and lean not on your own understanding; in all your ways acknowledge Him, and He shall direct your paths.

—PROVERBS 3:5–6

Simplicity is the only thing that can sufficiently reorient our lives so that possessions can be genuinely enjoyed without destroying us.

—RICHARD J. FOSTER

I Need to Simplify My Life

Dear God of Peace,

My life feels cluttered right now. My household is not in order. I can't find anything. I am working on many things and not doing any of them very well. I don't feel connected to friends and family because I am running so many different directions. I'm forgetting things and then showing up late!

I know, dear God, You are not the author of confusion. I know that the enemy of my soul would love to create so many distractions and worries that I forget to trust and love You. He would love nothing more than to rob me of my joy. He would love to see me lose my sense of priority.

But You are a God of peace! I turn to You right now for guidance on what things I need to hold tightly to, and what things I need to let go of. I have taken on too much and have become distracted by things that don't really matter. I know there are even some good activities I need to forgo in order that I do what's best. I know as I lean on You today that You will bring a new sense of order and peace to my life and to my household.

Thank You for peace.

In Jesus' name.

But those who wait on the Lord shall renew their strength;

they shall mount up with wings like eagles, they shall

run and not be weary, they shall walk and not faint.

—Isaiah 40:31 nkjv

And God is able to bless you abundantly, so that

in all things at all times, having all that you

need, you will abound in every good work.

—2 Corinthians 9:8 niv

It is so refreshing to know that we can rest in the strength

and comfort that God will provide when facing troubles of

many kinds. Let Him have the glory and show himself strong.

—Author Unknown

RENEW MY STRENGTH

O Mighty Lord,

I ask You for a renewed strength, vision, optimism, joyfulness, determination, courage, sense of humor, confidence, love, kindness, compassion, playfulness, faith, friendliness, gentleness, patience, and all the other dynamics that make me a light in the world.

I don't come to You defeated or discouraged—I just want to experience more of Your love and power. I want the energy and enthusiasm to live the abundant life that glorifies You and draws people toward knowing You.

Lord, just talking to You, spending time with You, waiting before You, already gives me a spark of vitality I did not feel before. Thank You for Your goodness to me. I receive Your love, grace, mercy, blessings, and empowerment with all humility and gratitude.

Thank You that with You working inside me I can do so much more than just get by—with Your strength, I can soar! All of this I pray with a grateful heart.

In Jesus' name.

"I have told you these things, so that in Me you may have [perfect] peace and confidence. In the world you have tribulation and trials and distress and frustration; but be of good cheer [take courage; be confident, certain, undaunted]! For I have overcome the world. [I have deprived it of power to harm you and have conquered it for you.]"

—JOHN 16:33 AMP

Who shall separate us from the love of Christ? Shall trouble or hardship or persecution or famine or nakedness or danger or sword? As it is written: "For your sake we face death all day long; we are considered as sheep to be slaughtered." No, in all these things we are more than conquerors through him who loved us. For I am convinced that neither death nor life, neither angels nor demons, neither the present nor the future, nor any powers, neither height nor depth, nor anything else in all creation, will be able to separate us from the love of God that is in Christ Jesus our Lord.

—ROMANS 8:35–39 NIV

*No matter how steep the mountain—
the Lord is going to climb it with you.*

—HELEN STEINER RICE

I Want to Overcome Adversity

Gracious God,

When life gets tough I find it too easy to complain, feel sorry for myself, and even quit. I live in a land of so many blessings that sometimes I lose that spirit of preparedness and fight that should characterize a person of strength and virtue.

I pray that I will always be mindful of the great love You have shown me through the sacrifice of Jesus Christ. As my great example of faith, He overcame all forms of suffering and temptation.

God, You are patient and kind, quick to forgive. Most of all, I want to honor You by being an overcomer. Thank You for giving me the help and strength I need whenever I face temptation and adversity of any kind.

In Jesus' mighty name.

Now the Lord said to Abram, "Go from your country and your kindred and your father's house to the land that I will show you. And I will make of you a great nation, and I will bless you and make your name great, so that you will be a blessing. I will bless those who bless you, and him who dishonors you I will curse, and in you all the families of the earth shall be blessed."

—GENESIS 12:1–3 ESV

"Have I not commanded you? Be strong and courageous. Do not be frightened, and do not be dismayed, for the Lord your God is with you wherever you go."

—JOSHUA 1:9 ESV

When one door closes, another opens, but we often look so long and so regretfully upon the closed door that we do not see the one that has opened for us.

—ALEXANDER GRAHAM BELL

I Am Moving

Faithful God,

I am getting ready to move. I am excited and realize this represents a new beginning and opportunity for me. But I am also nervous and even frightened. I feel a sense of loss leaving friends and familiar surroundings. I am stressed by the amount of planning and work that goes into moving from one home to another.

I trust You to take care of me in this journey of life. I know You will make my paths straight and ease the transition. Thank You. I pray in particular that You would help me find a new church and make new friends. I pray that the job (or school, or person) that brought about this move would bring the fulfillment I have anticipated.

Thank You that You never leave me nor forsake me—even as I travel to a new location in life.

In Jesus' name.

Let love and faithfulness never leave you; bind them around your neck, write them on the tablet of your heart. Then you will win favor and a good name in the sight of God and man.

—PROVERBS 3:3–4 NIV

A good name is more desirable than great riches; to be esteemed is better than silver or gold. Rich and poor have this in common: the Lord is the Maker of them all.

—PROVERBS 22:1–2 NIV

Of all the properties which belong to honorable men, not one is so highly prized as that of character.

—HENRY CLAY

MY REPUTATION

Righteous God,

When we are honest, fair, loyal, and kind we attain favor from the people in our lives, and most of all, from You. I pray these attributes would season all my relationships and all my business dealings that I would be known as a person of high character. I pray that my reputation will bring honor and glory to Your name.

If I have taken some ethical shortcuts and not shown character in my dealings with others, I pray for wisdom and strength to do all I can to set things right. Help me to apologize gracefully. Help me to make restitution. Help me own up to any dishonesty.

You call us to be different so that we can make a difference in the world. I want my reputation to be a beacon of how You have made me into a new and different person.

Thank You for correcting me and helping me to mature and grow when I stumble. May my thoughts, words, and deeds honor You, God of righteousness.

In Jesus' holy name.

Beware of false prophets, who come to you in sheep's clothing but inwardly are ravenous wolves.
—MATTHEW 7:15 ESV

But there were also false prophets among the people, just as there will be false teachers among you. They will secretly introduce destructive heresies, even denying the sovereign Lord who bought them— bringing swift destruction on themselves.
—2 PETER 2:1 NIV

Nothing makes a man so virtuous as belief of the truth. A lying doctrine will soon beget a lying practice. A man cannot have an erroneous belief without by-and-by having an erroneous life. I believe the one thing naturally begets the other.
—CHARLES SPURGEON

I Need Protection
from False Teachings

Dear God,

We live in a day of spiritual confusion. There are thousands of voices who claim to know truth and the way to peace, happiness, and eternal life. Many of these teachers do not know nor acknowledge that You are the one true God, who is alone worthy to be praised.

In times of crisis, false teachers will prey on those who are not strong in their faith, who are not familiar with Your Word. I pray that You will raise up men and women who will boldly proclaim the truth of Jesus Christ. I pray that You will protect the innocent and gullible from wolves in sheep's clothing.

God, I pray that I will always be able to give a reason for the hope that lies within me. I pray that I will not be tossed back and forth by waves of false teaching. I pray that I will continue to grow in wisdom and faith; that I will be mature and complete, lacking in nothing of spiritual value

In Jesus' matchless name.

"Come to me, all of you who are weary and carry heavy burdens, and I will give you rest. Take my yoke upon you and you will find rest for your souls. For my yoke fits perfectly, and the burden I give you is light."
—MATTHEW 11:28–30 NLT

Give all your worries and cares to God, for he cares about you.
—1 PETER 5:7 NLT

What can be lighter than a burden which takes our burdens away, and a yoke which bears up the bearer himself?
—ST. BERNARD

I Have a Burden I Can't Handle

O Lord of All Comfort,

You know the burden I am carrying right now. I don't come to complain or feel sorry for myself. I just need to let You know that I don't feel I can carry this weight anymore. I come to You with a sense of weariness. I'm not sure how I can keep going.

Thank You for inviting me to bring my burdens to You. Thank You for letting me be honest about how I feel and my temptation to give up. Thank You for having the empathy to know that I am struggling to positively express faith and hope right now. Thank You for Your promise that You will give me whatever strength I need for the challenges of each day—even if I don't feel very strong right now.

I am humbled and grateful that You still accept and embrace me as I am, and that You offer to carry my load with me. I don't know how to put this in Your hands, but in my heart and spirit I give You my burden now.

O Lord, just knowing that You are close to me right now gives hope to my soul.

In the name of the Lord.

"I do believe; help me overcome my unbelief!"

—**MARK 9:24** NIV

Now Thomas (also known as Didymus), one of the
Twelve, was not with the disciples when Jesus came.
So the other disciples told him, "We have seen the
Lord!" But he said to them, "Unless I see the nail marks
in his hands and put my finger where the nails were,
and put my hand into his side, I will not believe."

—**JOHN 20:24–25** NIV

There lives more faith in honest doubt,
believe me, than in half the creeds.

—**ALFRED LORD TENNYSON**

I HAVE DOUBTS

Faithful Lord,

It is hard to come to You in prayer when I have doubts in my heart. But I know You call me to come to You with all my needs. You welcomed the Apostle Thomas when he doubted Your resurrection, and You showed him your nail-pierced hands. And You welcome me.

I need to see You and feel Your presence. I have faith but it is weak. I need a renewed sense that You and Your truth are real.

There is so much skepticism and cynicism in the world I live in and I get caught up in that. I pray that You would help me resist the temptations of scoffers and critics.

I pray right now that You would transform and renew my mind as I offer myself to You in simple faith. Thank You for Your love for me. Help me to cling to that when I am buffeted by waves of doubt.

In Jesus' precious name.

A cheerful heart is good medicine.

—**PROVERBS 17:22 NLT**

I will greatly rejoice in the Lord, my soul shall be joyful in my God; for He has clothed me with the garments of salvation, He has covered me with the robe of righteousness.

—**ISAIAH 61:10 NKJV**

If I am not allowed to laugh in heaven,
I don't want to go there.

—**MARTIN LUTHER**

I Need Joy and Laughter

God of Grace,

I know there is much to be serious about in life, but I am afraid I have become too heavy and serious about everything. I'm not fun to be around. I feel critical when I see others enjoying themselves. I have forgotten that You are the God of joy and laughter.

Thank You for creating us to experience joy and laughter. Thank You that You have called for us to celebrate as members of Your Kingdom. Jesus Christ knew how to have fun and laugh—and was even criticized for it by religious leaders. So I know You want me to know when it is time to be sober, respectful, caring, and appropriately serious—but You also invite me to cut loose, to celebrate, to smile and laugh at the humor and levity of life!

Today, help me to remember that You are God—and You have everything under control. I'm not going to worry, judge, or walk around with a scowl on my face. I'm going to laugh at jokes—and even tell a few of my own. I am going to experience the joy and happiness of knowing You love me and hold me safely in Your hands.

In Your grace, I am going to be a witness of the joyful life You give as I smile at the world.

In Jesus' wonderful name.

*"But seek first his kingdom and his righteousness,
and all these things will be given to you as well."*
—**MATTHEW 6:33 NIV**

*"Whoever wants to be my disciple must deny themselves
and take up their cross daily and follow me. For whoever
wants to save their life will lose it, but whoever loses their
life for me will save it. What good is it for someone to gain
the whole world, and yet lose or forfeit their very self?"*
—**LUKE 9:23–25 NIV**

*If we are to go forward, we must go back and rediscover
those precious values—that all reality hinges on moral
foundations and that all reality has spiritual control.*
—**MARTIN LUTHER KING, JR.**

I Need to Change My Priorities

God of Wisdom,

I have lost my way. I'm off-track. My values aren't where they should be. I have fallen in love with the wrong things. I'm not spiritually minded. My priorities are a mess. I don't like what I've created out of my life right now.

I have no answers on how to straighten things out. So I come to You in humility. I ask for Your forgiveness. I want You to know that I do love You even though it hasn't seemed that way for a long time. I want to draw close to You again. I pray that You would accept me into Your presence like the loving father accepted the Prodigal Son.

Place in me a new heart, O God. Help me to love what You love, to hate what You hate, to prioritize what You prioritize. I want You and Your ways to be first priority in my life. I will hold fast to Your promise that if I seek You and Your kingdom first, everything else in life will fall in place. I want that and pray for that with all my heart right now.

Thank You for Your kindness and correction, God. Thank You for making me aware of my need for You and for giving my priorities to You.

In Jesus' name.

For unto us a Child is born, Unto us a Son is given;

And the government will be upon His shoulder.

And His name will be called Wonderful, Counselor,

Mighty God, Everlasting Father, Prince of Peace.

—ISAIAH 9:6 NKJV

And suddenly there was with the angel a multitude of the

heavenly host praising God and saying: "Glory to God in

the highest, and on earth peace, goodwill toward men!"

—LUKE 2:13–14 NKJV

Christmas, my child, is love in action. Every time

we love, every time we give, it's Christmas.

—DALE EVANS

A Prayer at Christmas

God of Joy,

The holidays are approaching and I look forward to special times with friends and family; to celebrating Your love and goodness to us. Thank You so much for giving us the gift of Jesus. Help me to have a heart filled with gratitude and praise as I am reminded of that glorious night so long ago.

Many people do not look forward to Christmas and experience depression and feelings of aloneness. You know who I have in my heart and mind. Give me grace to reach out to them with kindness and encouragement.

Some people are unhappy during the Christmas season because they don't know You and are still resisting Your grace. They seem to fight the Spirit of Christmas. I pray that even the rebellious would feel the wonder of the story—and truth—of Christmas.

Bless my friends and loved ones. Give us cherished moments together that we will never forget.

In Jesus' name.

I know what it is to be in need, and I know what it is to have plenty. I have learned the secret of being content in any and every situation, whether well fed or hungry, whether living in plenty or in want.

—PHILIPPIANS 4:12 NIV

Yes, everything else is worthless when compared with the priceless gain of knowing Christ Jesus my Lord. I have discarded everything else, counting it all as garbage, so that I may have Christ.

—PHILIPPIANS 3:8 NLT

Seek every day to have closer communion with Him who is your Friend, and to know more of His grace and power. True Christianity is not merely believing a certain set of dry abstract propositions: it is to live in daily personal communication with an actual living person—Jesus Christ.

—J. C. RYLE

I Want to Draw Closer to God

Dear Heavenly Father,

Whether my life is easy or hard; whether things are going my way or uncertain; I pray that in all seasons of life my greatest desire will be to grow closer to You. Don't let success or failure take my eyes off of You and what matters most in life. I don't want to ever drift away from You and lose my love for You. God, You know that I have faith, but I pray that You would help my faith to grow even stronger and greater.

When life seems easier and comfortable, it is tempting for me to drift in my spiritual walk; to believe somehow that I have things under control and don't need Your help quite as much. When life is difficult, I know I have sometimes succumbed to the temptation of discouragement. I don't want to be a person of weak faith.

Today I want to draw near to You, knowing full well You will draw near to me. I confess my absolute dependence on You. I declare that nothing I possess, no accomplishment or ability, can compare to the privilege and joy of knowing You even better.

I thank You right now that You are strengthening me in my faith.

In Jesus' name.

So I find this law at work: Although I want to do good, evil is right there with me. For in my inner being I delight in God's law; but I see another law at work in me, waging war against the law of my mind and making me a prisoner of the law of sin at work within me. What a wretched man I am! Who will rescue me from this body that is subject to death? Thanks be to God, who delivers me through Jesus Christ our Lord!

—ROMANS 7:21–25 NIV

"Watch and pray so that you will not fall into temptation. The spirit is willing, but the flesh is weak."

—MATTHEW 26:41 NIV

Every moment of resistance to temptation is a victory.

—FREDERICK WILLIAM FABER

THE ONE SIN

God of Salvation,

You know the one sin that is a plague on my spiritual life and that I seemingly cannot overcome.

I have prayed to You before for relief, but it always comes back. I have tried to keep busy and find other ways to ignore it but it seems to be my constant companion. My spirit is willing but my flesh is weak.

I am at a loss. I do not know what to do. You know I love You and want to feel Your presence in every area of my life, but this sin embarrasses me before You and makes me feel like You can no longer love me. It makes me feel miserable about myself.

I am desperate. What can I do O God?

I pray that You would not turn me away. I submit to Your will and Your ways on dealing with this. I don't want to rationalize and accept sin in my life, but if this is going to take time to be resolved, I pray for grace to ask forgiveness as many times as necessary to enjoy Your fellowship.

Even as the Apostle Paul prayed for deliverance from his infirmity, I will continue to pray for Your complete deliverance and total victory.

In Jesus' name.

You were running a good race. Who cut in on you to keep you from obeying the truth? That kind of persuasion does not come from the one who calls you. "A little yeast works through the whole batch of dough." I am confident in the Lord that you will take no other view. The one who is throwing you into confusion, whoever that may be, will have to pay the penalty.

—Galatians 5:7–10 niv

Keep watch over yourselves and all the flock of which the Holy Spirit has made you overseers. Be shepherds of the church of God, which he bought with his own blood.

—Acts 20:28 niv

The church is a perpetually defeated thing that always survives her conquerors.

—Hilaire Belloc

My Church Is Falling Apart

Merciful Father,

My church is not doing well. There is strife and major disagreement. People are quitting and going to other churches or just not going to church at all. Those who do come look unhappy and bored. I don't see a spirit of love and service. I'm not sure a visitor would feel welcome here. Even our pastor looks discouraged.

Father in Heaven, I am not a quitter. I don't want to leave my church. I want to stay and see things turn around. I want to see revival where we love one another again and find ways to reach our neighborhood and world with your gospel. But Father, I also admit that I need to be part of a fellowship where I am fed spiritually.

So would You help me know what Your will is for me? I need Your guidance and for Your Spirit to speak to my heart.

If You want me to stay, I will do all in my power to build up this body of Christ. If I stay, help me to gain spiritual encouragement through books and videos and a Bible study or other fellowship group. If You release me to look for another church help me to find a place where Your Word is proclaimed and I have opportunities for both fellowship and service.

Thank You that even when the church is weak and struggling it is still the church when You are present.

In Jesus' name.

*But one thing I do: Forgetting what is behind
and straining toward what is ahead, I press on
toward the goal to win the prize for which God
has called me heavenward in Christ Jesus.*

—Philippians 3:13–14 NIV

*And let us not grow weary while doing good, for in
due season we shall reap if we do not lose heart.*

—Galatians 6:9 NKJV

Never, never, never give up.

—Winston Churchill

I Won't Give Up

Dear Lord,

Even if my friends forsake me . . . I won't give up.

Even if my children go through a period of rebelliousness . . . I won't give up.

Even if my spouse and I struggle for a season . . . I won't give up.

Even if my church experiences problems and strife . . . I won't give up.

Even if my own life doesn't measure up to what You expect from me and what I expect from myself . . . I won't give up.

You have helped me to plant seeds of faith and grace. And You have promised that if I persist, if I don't give up, there will be a great harvest in the right season.

Lord, great days are ahead. I'm not quitting now!

MY WORLD
AND NATION

The preaching that this world needs
most is the sermons in shoes that are
walking with Jesus Christ.
—D. L. MOODY

Blessed is the nation whose God is the Lord,

the people he chose for his inheritance.

—PSALM 33:12 NIV

For the grace of God has appeared that offers salvation

to all people. It teaches us to say "No" to ungodliness

and worldly passions, and to live self-controlled, upright

and godly lives in this present age, while we wait for the

blessed hope—the appearing of the glory of our great

God and Savior, Jesus Christ, who gave himself for us to

redeem us from all wickedness and to purify for himself a

people that are his very own, eager to do what is good.

—TITUS 2:11–14 NIV

It is a fact that unless children are brought up in the

nurture and admonition of the Lord, they, and the society

which they constitute or control, will go to destruction.

Consequently, when a state resolves that religious instruction

shall be banished from the schools and other literary

institutions, it virtually resolves on self-destruction.

—CHARLES HODGE

BLESS MY COUNTRY

Father God,

I thank You for all the blessings that are mine through living in this great country. I thank You for a rich history that includes political leaders and people from all walks of life recognizing that You are the giver of all good gifts: liberty, prosperity, justice, opportunity, security, and all other good things that make a nation great.

In our profane and godless entertainment, in the decisions in our courtrooms, in the laws enacted in our legislature, in our lack of ethical business dealings, in our lack of compassion, in our loss of civility, in our lack of morality, I fear my country has lost its way spiritually. Your name is not lifted up. We have taken credit for our success and blessings and don't have the humility to acknowledge our need for You.

First of all, I humbly pray that You would forgive all my sins and keep me from all wicked paths. Then I humbly pray that You would stir the hearts of fellow believers to pray that same prayer of personal renewal with me. Finally, I pray that by humbly seeking You and Your ways we would spark a revival that reaches millions with the truth of the Gospel—and that revival will make this a nation great in faith.

Has not the one God made you? You belong to him in body and spirit. And what does the one God seek? Godly offspring. So be on your guard, and do not be unfaithful to the wife of your youth. "The man who hates and divorces his wife," says the Lord, the God of Israel, "does violence to the one he should protect," says the Lord Almighty. So be on your guard, and do not be unfaithful.

—Malachi 2:15–16 niv

"He will turn the hearts of the parents to their children, and the hearts of the children to their parents; or else I will come and strike the land with total destruction."

—Malachi 4:6 niv

There aren't any easy answers to the questions being raised today, and it may be too easy for me to remember Jesus saying, "Greater love has no man than to give up his life for his friend." Or wife; or children. Isn't staying with your family sometimes a real equivalent of giving up your own life? Cannot it sometimes be a blessing, especially if it is given with graciousness, not rigid rectitude?

—Madeleine L'Engle

Strengthen Marriages and Families

Heavenly Father,

The divorce rate and number of broken families in my nation and around the world is staggering. The cost of broken homes is staggering as well, which can be measured in dollars and cents, but even more so in the trauma and tragedy experienced by children and adults alike.

There are so many messages from experts and the entertainment industry that don't encourage family unity, but instead seem to glorify the seeds of family destruction, from promiscuity and infidelity to ignoring or downplaying the true price we pay for divorce and family dissolution.

I pray that You would stir the hearts of husbands and wives and that they would turn to You and to each other. I pray the love between parents and children would be kindled and grow in both directions.

I pray that You would lift a hand of protection against those who would speak against and seek to damage families. I ask that You would restore my country's commitment to supporting and affirming the importance of strong family values.

When You created the world You created families. I pray for family unity in the world and my nation—beginning in my home.

In Jesus' name.

Therefore I exhort first of all that supplications, prayers,

intercessions, and giving of thanks be made for all men,

for kings and all who are in authority, that we may lead a

quiet and peaceable life in all godliness and reverence.

—1 Timothy 2:1–2 nkjv

The fear of the Lord is the beginning of wisdom;

a good understanding have all those who do His

commandments. His praise endures forever.

—Psalm 111:10 nkjv

Nearly all men can stand adversity, but if you want

to test a man's character, give him power.

—Abraham Lincoln

GIVE WISDOM TO OUR LEADERS

Dear Mighty God,

You provide guidance, protection, and order in our world through leaders. Not all authority figures live according to Your will and ways—and You tell us that our first obedience and allegiance is to You. Yet You call for us to submit to authorities.

Mighty God, I ask You to forgive me for the times when I am rebellious and resistant with leadership. Sometimes I simply do not want to follow the lead of those in positions of authority and want my own way. Thank You that You will build my character and my own strength through my willingness to submit.

Mighty God, in a world filled with challenges, our nation's leaders need our support and prayers more than ever. I pray You would help our leaders realize their need for You and Your guidance in their personal and public life. Teach me the lessons as I do my best to be a great follower. Help me to be a leader in my attitude toward the president, congress, the military, and leaders at every level of government and business. I will serve You as I serve my leaders.

In Jesus' mighty name.

But Stephen, full of the Holy Spirit, looked up to heaven and saw the glory of God, and Jesus standing at the right hand of God. "Look," he said, "I see heaven open and the Son of Man standing at the right hand of God." . . . While they were stoning him, Stephen prayed, "Lord Jesus, receive my spirit." Then he fell on his knees and cried out, "Lord, do not hold this sin against them." When he had said this, he fell asleep.

—ACTS 7:55–56,59–60 NIV

"Then you will be handed over to be persecuted and put to death, and you will be hated by all nations because of me. At that time many will turn away from the faith and will betray and hate each other, and many false prophets will appear and deceive many people. Because of the increase of wickedness, the love of most will grow cold, but the one who stands firm to the end will be saved. And this gospel of the kingdom will be preached in the whole world as a testimony to all nations, and then the end will come."

—MATTHEW 24:9–14 NIV

But, though persecuting malice raged, yet the Gospel shone with resplendent brightness; and, firm as an impregnable rock, withstood the attacks of its boisterous enemies with success.

—JOHN FOXE

THOSE BEING PERSECUTED FOR CHRIST

Righteous King,

No generation has had more Christian martyrs and greater persecution than this present one. I confess that because I am not in danger personally I forget about suffering Christians in other parts of the world. I live in a country where the worst that can happen to me for being a Christian is perhaps being made fun of or some social discrimination. But I don't experience what my brothers and sisters in faith are going through in many parts of the world, particularly in the Middle East and Asia.

I ask for Your protection on those under persecution now. The Apostle Paul says that to live is Christ but to die is gain. And I know that Heaven will be a relief and a wonderful place for those who have been martyred. But we are still to pray for God's will on earth as it is in heaven. I pray that my nation would attempt to exercise more pressure for those under persecution with international bodies and directly with countries that are doing the persecution. Help my country to be a force for justice on behalf of any groups that are singled out for mistreatment because of their faith.

Thank You that I live in a country that is established on religious liberty. Help us to never compromise nor lose that.

I pray that I would remain mindful of those who are under persecution and exercise what influence I have to help them.

In Jesus' merciful name.

If my people, who are called by my name, will humble themselves and pray and seek my face and turn from their wicked ways, then I will hear from heaven, and I will forgive their sin and will heal their land.

—2 CHRONICLES 7:14 NIV

Where there is no prophetic vision the people cast off restraint, but blessed is he who keeps the law.

—PROVERBS 29:18 ESV

There is a famine in America. Not a famine of food, but of love, of truth, of life.

—MOTHER TERESA

Renew My Country Spiritually

Dear God in Heaven,

You know the condition of our world. You know the state of our nation. We are so blessed, so wealthy, so advanced, so good and generous. But You also know the dark side of our land. Infidelity, broken families, greed, corruption, abuse, and countless forms of immorality dominate our landscape.

So many people are resistant to hearing Your Truth and giving You honor for all You have done to bless us. They fight any mention of Your name in schools and the public square. They promote immorality and false teachings.

I pray that there would be a revival in my country. I pray that millions more hearts would turn to You. Teach us to be humble and to pray. Help us to turn from any ways that are not pleasing to You. I pray that we would repent of sinful ways and live for You so that righteousness would flow in our land.

I pray that You would forgive and heal my nation—and that You would begin that work in me.

Thomas said to him, "Lord, we don't know where you are going, so how can we know the way?" Jesus answered, "I am the way and the truth and the life. No one comes to the Father except through me. If you really know me, you will know my Father as well. From now on, you do know him and have seen him."

—JOHN 14:5–7 NIV

Do your best to present yourself to God as one approved, a worker who does not need to be ashamed and who correctly handles the word of truth.

—2 TIMOTHY 2:15 NIV

In essentials, unity; in differences, liberty; in all things, charity.

—PHILIPP MELANCHTHON

HELP ME UPHOLD THE TRUTH

Holy God,

It is hard to know and walk in Your truth in this current age. There are so many competing ideas and philosophies, even within Your church. I don't want to argue over every detail of theology or every interpretation of Scripture, but I do want to hold fast to the essentials of the Christian faith. Salvation by the death and resurrection of Jesus Christ. The authority of Your Word. The universal need for salvation.

I pray that You would protect me—and the entire church of Jesus Christ—from false teachings. I pray we would not fall for wolves dressed in sheep's clothing. I pray that we would not be ensnared with a false gospel that is not built on the teachings of Jesus Christ as revealed in Your Word.

I don't want to be contentious or judgmental in regard to people who see things differently than me, but I do want to stand up and positively support sound teaching and theology. Give me the wisdom to hold my tongue when a difference of opinion is not essential to the faith, but to speak positively and boldly when truths about who You are and our need for You come into question.

Thank You for speaking clearly to us on matters of salvation.

In Jesus' name.

From one man he made all the nations, that they should inhabit the whole earth; and he marked out their appointed times in history and the boundaries of their lands. God did this so that they would seek him and perhaps reach out for him and find him, though he is not far from any one of us.

—ACTS 17:26–27 NIV

For you are all children of God through faith in Christ Jesus. And all who have been united with Christ in baptism have put on Christ, like putting on new clothes. There is no longer Jew or Gentile, slave or free, male and female. For you are all one in Christ Jesus.

—GALATIANS 3:26–28 NLT

Jesus Christ didn't die on the cross for one race or one nation; He died for the whole world.

—BILLY GRAHAM

Establish Racial Harmony

Creator God,

You love everyone in the world. You are no respecter of race or color. All individuals are of infinite worth and value in Your eyes. You gave Your life for the sins of everyone in the world. I pray that I would always look at people the same way that You do.

It seems that our nation is having internal strife over race to an increased degree. I don't know if this is a manufactured conflict by people who are using race for political ends or if there truly is more racism in our country than before. Whatever is true, my prayer is the same. Help us to unite around shared values and goals and ignore color of skin and ethnic background as the measures of how we judge a person. Judgments on actions are inevitable, but not superficial issues of skin tone.

If people are fanning flames of distrust and dislike, I pray You would raise Your hand to stop them. I pray that people from every race and background would feel Your love and their worth in Your eyes and would pursue all opportunities You plant in their heart without fear.

You are the prince of peace and we ask for racial peace now.

In Jesus' name.

When times are good, you should be cheerful; when
times are bad, think what it means. God makes them
both to keep us from knowing what will happen next.
—ECCLESIASTES 7:14 CEV

The Lord is good, a Strength and Stronghold in the day
of trouble; He knows (recognizes, has knowledge of,
and understands) those who take refuge and trust in Him.
—NAHUM 1:7 AMP

If we abide by the principles taught in the Bible,
our country will go on prospering and to prosper. I make
it a practice to read the Bible through once every year.
—DANIEL WEBSTER

STRENGTHEN MY COUNTRY'S ECONOMY

Father God,

All blessings come from You individually and corporately—including the blessings of nations. My country has been blessed in so many ways. We have a tremendous farmland and our people are fed. We are rich in natural resources. From highways to energy to commerce we have a powerful infrastructure. We have long had a strong middle class and millions have prospered to even greater levels.

But I am afraid we have taken these blessings for granted and given all the credit to our own efforts. Now that our economy has languished in a prolonged downturn, people are angry and resentful. Fingers are pointed every which way as to who is to blame.

I do pray for our economy to get back on track so that unemployment drops dramatically and people are able to meet their financial obligations. I do pray for millions of individuals unemployed or underemployed who are struggling. But I pray there would be a spiritual renewal that accompanies this—with more gratitude and less foolish pride, greed, and grievance. Even greater than our need for a robust economy is our need to know and honor You.

Even as our economy struggles and turns around, I pray that this nation would not forget the destitute of the world and that as individuals and a country we would continue to be generous in our help.

In Jesus' name.

And He said to them, "Go into all the world and preach the gospel to every creature. He who believes and is baptized will be saved; but he who does not believe will be condemned."
—MARK 16:15–16 NKJV

"For the Son of Man came to seek and to save the lost."
—LUKE 19:10 NIV

I am a missionary, heart and soul. God had an only Son, and he was a missionary and a physician. A poor, poor imitation of him I am, or wish to be. In this service I hope to live; in it I wish to die.
—DAVID LIVINGSTONE

A Lost and Dying World

God of Love,

I pray that the command You have given us to take the gospel to the farthest parts of the world will be fulfilled in this age. I pray that Your servants will find creative ways to reach people who have never heard the gospel. I pray that You will continue to raise up missionaries, translators, and those who work overseas in order to share the gospel. I pray that there would be financial support so that no opportunity is missed because there were not adequate funds.

There are people in every nook and cranny of the world who have never heard the gospel—including in my own country and neighborhood—and there are millions upon millions more who have not responded. I pray that those who are called Christians—and not everyone that goes by that name truly knows You—will walk worthy of that name so that no one will reject the gospel because of the attitudes and actions of those who are called Christians.

As the whole world is reached with the gospel I pray that there would be renewal in countries that used to be Christian but are now dominated by skepticism.

Show me how I can be used to reach the world with Your love.

In Jesus' blessed name.

The Lord will open to you His good treasure, the heavens, to give the rain to your land in its season, and to bless all the work of your hand. You shall lend to many nations, but you shall not borrow.

—DEUTERONOMY 28:12 NKJV

Enter his gates with thanksgiving and his courts with praise; give thanks to him and praise his name. For the Lord is good and his love endures forever; his faithfulness continues through all generations.

—PSALM 100:4–5 NIV

It cannot be emphasized too strongly or too often that this great nation was founded not by religionists, but by Christians; not on religions, but on the gospel of Jesus Christ. For that reason alone, people of other faiths have been afforded freedom of worship here.

—PATRICK HENRY

I Am Thankful for My Country

Dear Lord,

You are a good, kind, faithful, loving God. Your mercies are new every morning. You give us strength to handle every challenge that we face. You are the giver of all good gifts and blessings.

One of the greatest blessings in my life is the country that I live in. When I look at all the nations of the world, I realize anew that it is a country of prosperity and generosity; of strength and safety; of opportunity and work; of law and grace.

Your hand has been on this land since the day it was born. And I know that Your hand will be on my country in the future if we honor You. I pray that You will renew in my heart a sense of gratitude for this great nation. Help me to never take my country for granted or to ignore any of Your other blessings on my life. I continue to pray for spiritual renewal in my country. So many people want to diminish Your role in this land and give the credit to humans. But the ones who have made the biggest difference in our country have given You the credit. So help me to confidently proclaim your goodness and good works.

Today I come into Your presence with thanksgiving and praise. I rejoice in You. I declare Your faithfulness. And I thank You that You have blessed me so much to be a citizen of this land.

Surely he will save you from the fowler's snare and from the deadly pestilence. He will cover you with his feathers, and under his wings you will find refuge; his faithfulness will be your shield and rampart. You will not fear the terror of night, nor the arrow that flies by day, nor the pestilence that stalks in the darkness, nor the plague that destroys at midday. A thousand may fall at your side, ten thousand at your right hand, but it will not come near you.

—PSALM 91:3–7 NIV

"Peace I leave with you; my peace I give you. I do not give to you as the world gives. Do not let your hearts be troubled and do not be afraid."

—JOHN 14:27 NIV

The reason why many fail in battle is because they wait until the hour of battle. The reason why others succeed is because they have gained their victory on their knees long before the battle came.

—REUBEN ARCHER TORREY

PROTECT OUR SOLDIERS

Dear Heavenly Father,

I pray first and foremost for peace among nations and peoples.

When there is war, I pray for protection for the men and women of our military. You said in Your Word that You would never leave us nor forsake us. I believe that Your angels go before our soldiers to protect them and keep them from harm and danger of any kind.

Lord, Your Word says that You hide us under Your wings, that no evil shall befall us, and that no plague or calamity shall come near our homes. I pray for safety over each military operation. Wherever our troops go and whatever they do, I thank You that they operate in Your divine protection. I pray for safety as they travel by air, sea, and land to every destination. I pray that You protect them from the enemy, friendly fire, or mere accidents. I pray that You protect them from any threats of physical, mental, or emotional violence.

Father, I pray for Your peace that passes all understanding. May it guard the hearts and minds of our soldiers. Thank You for Your protection in every area of their lives.

In Jesus' mighty name.

Pray for the peace of Jerusalem: "May they prosper who love you. Peace be within your walls, prosperity within your palaces."

—PSALM 122:6–7 NKJV

"Who will not fear you, Lord, and bring glory to your name? For you alone are holy. All nations will come and worship before you, for your righteous acts have been revealed."

—REVELATION 15:4 NIV

Let there be peace on earth, and let it begin with me.

—SONG LYRICS

PRAYER FOR THE MIDDLE EAST

God of Peace,

Nowhere in the world is there more hatred, conflict, and fighting than the Middle East. The battles brewing and already being fought there transcend geography and are ready to spill into all areas of our world.

Even if I don't understand all the nuances of biblical prophecy, even if I don't understand all the politics of the region, I can pray with all my heart for Your peace in the Holy Land. I pray that Your wisdom would prevail, even with those who don't know You. I pray that hatred would be replaced by good will, that swords would be beaten into plough shares.

Many people don't believe in witnessing to people of other faiths, but I do believe that Jesus Christ is the way, the truth, and the light—and that when people are saved and serve Him with all their heart, the world changes for the better. I believe He is the hope of the world. So I pray that there would be a true revival in the Middle East and that millions would come to know Your saving grace.

Protect my country's citizens, soldiers, and interests that are in the region.

In the name of Jesus, the Prince of Peace.

Choose some well-respected men from each tribe
who are known for their wisdom and understanding,
and I will appoint them as your leaders.

—**DEUTERONOMY 1:13 NLT**

Everyone must submit to governing authorities. For
all authority comes from God, and those in positions
of authority have been placed there by God.

—**ROMANS 13:1 NLT**

The authority by which the Christian leader leads is not
power but love, not force but example, not coercion but
reasoned persuasion. Leaders have power, but power is safe
only in the hands of those who humble themselves to serve.

—**JOHN STOTT**

GIVE US WISE AND GODLY LEADERS

Mighty God,

In families, communities, churches, organizations, companies—
and nations—success seems to rise and fall with the quality
of leadership.

We need great leaders at every level of society and organization,
men and women of wisdom, grace, poise, self-sacrifice, and courage.
The founders of this nation sacrificed much personal gain and were
always ready to give You all the glory for success, and that's just the
kind of leaders we need today.

I know there is no perfect leader to solve all problems, but I
ask that You give this nation mayors, representatives, senators,
judges, governors, and president that strengthen the fabric of our
country because they honor You. Help them to flee from corruption. Protect their spirit of service from the temptations of cynicism
and arrogance.

We welcome people of all faiths if they are law-abiding and of
good will. We know You work in the hearts of the faithful but even
in the hearts of nonbelievers to restrain evil and encourage good.

I pray You would encourage goodness in our leaders today.

In the name of Jesus Christ I pray.

All of you, clothe yourselves with humility toward one another, because, "God opposes the proud but shows favor to the humble." Humble yourselves, therefore, under God's mighty hand, that he may lift you up in due time.

—1 PETER 5:5–6 NIV

If a kingdom is divided against itself, that kingdom cannot stand. And if a house is divided against itself, that house cannot stand.

—MARK 3:24–25 NKJV

America will never be destroyed from the outside. If we falter and lose our freedoms, it will be because we destroyed ourselves.

—ABRAHAM LINCOLN

Restore Unity in Our Nation

God of Peace,

My country is so divided right now. There are so many grievances and complaints on the basis of race, financial status, political
affiliation, age, gender, and so much more. So many people—on all
sides of the issues—feel they are not being given justice. There seems
to be a tremendous loss of the common goals and vision that once
united us.

I believe the entire world is blessed when my country is strong
and united. I ask that Your Spirit would travel throughout this land,
raising up true leaders of integrity that can communicate Your
values and vision. I pray that rather than rebelling and resisting You
would place in people's heart the willingness to listen to and follow
good counsel and direction. There is so much rebelliousness right
now that we need a real turnaround.

When we honor You we are lifted up, so I pray that there would
be a revival in the land, that couples and families would be strengthened. Let unity begin in the home.

All this I pray in Jesus' name.

May his name endure forever; may it continue as long as the sun. Then all nations will be blessed through him, and they will call him blessed. Praise be to the Lord God, the God of Israel, who alone does marvelous deeds. Praise be to his glorious name forever; may the whole earth be filled with his glory. Amen and Amen.

—PSALM 72:17–19 NIV

In the same way, the gospel is bearing fruit and growing throughout the whole world—just as it has been doing among you since the day you heard it and truly understood God's grace.

—COLOSSIANS 1:6 NIV

Today, we utter no prayer more fervently than the ancient prayer for peace on Earth.

—RONALD REAGAN

Use My Country to Bless the World

Heavenly Father,

In the name of Jesus, I pray for the international relations of my nation. I pray that You would cause us to have favor with the other nations of the earth. I pray that we would be fair and effective in treaties. I pray the freedoms and prosperity we enjoy would spill over to other countries. I pray that we would continue to be generous in helping meet humanitarian needs. I pray You would protect us from the schemes of evil regimes that mean to harm us, our allies, and anyone that does not agree with them.

I pray that because of our international influence, doors would open in nations that have been closed to the gospel in the past. I pray that You continue to call people of all ages to share Your good news around the world. Please grant favor to the missionaries in their respective nations, particularly where there is danger in being an ambassador for Christ.

Raise up wise men and women to fill our diplomatic corps, persons of skill and understanding in foreign affairs, with loyalty to our country and goodwill for all.

Grant favor to our embassy personnel on every foreign front, so they will be able to maintain good relations in their respective posts and so that even our enemies will be at peace with them. Give them safety.

All this I pray in the name of the Prince of Peace.

"But you will receive power when the Holy Spirit has come upon you, and you will be my witnesses in Jerusalem and in all Judea and Samaria, and to the end of the earth."
—**ACTS 1:8** ESV

How then will they call on him in whom they have not believed? And how are they to believe in him of whom they have never heard? And how are they to hear without someone preaching? And how are they to preach unless they are sent? As it is written, "How beautiful are the feet of those who preach the good news!"
—**ROMANS 10:14–15** ESV

We are all missionaries . . . wherever we go, we either bring people nearer to Christ, or we repel them from Christ.
—**ERIC LIDDELL**

HELP ME SPEAK THE GOOD NEWS

Dear God,

You are kind and gracious, slow to anger. Even when we have sinned and rebelled against You, Your desire is not to condemn us, but to save us through your Son, Jesus Christ. You love us so much that even though we have acted as Your enemy, You sent Jesus to die for our sins.

God, thank You for that amazing love that is alive in my own life. And I pray, dear God, that I will never be satisfied to just experience Your love for myself, but will pass that love on to others.

God, there are people all around me who seem resistant to You, the gospel, and Your church. Deep down they may be searching for answers—but it is very hard to bring up spiritual matters with them. You have put people in my path because I can make a difference in their life.

Would You give me the sensitivity to know who is ready to hear about Your grace and salvation? Would You help me be ready to share how You have made my life brand new? Would You give me the perfect words to explain how to be saved? Would You create the opportunities for spiritual conversation and prayer to take place?

God, I am not ashamed of Your gospel and will tell the world of Your goodness!

If you say, "The Lord is my refuge," and you make the Most High your dwelling, no harm will overtake you, no disaster will come near your tent.

—PSALM 91:9–10 NIV

"You will be secure under a government that is just and fair. Your enemies will stay far away. You will live in peace, and terror will not come near. If any nation comes to fight you, it is not because I sent them. Whoever attacks you will go down in defeat."

—ISAIAH 54:14–15 NLT

It is the duty of all nations to acknowledge the providence of Almighty God, to obey his will, to be grateful for his benefits, and humbly to implore his protection and favor.

—GEORGE WASHINGTON

Keep My Country Safe

Dear God of Protection,

I pray for the safety of my country, that You would protect us from any attack on our soil. I pray this protection from enemies within or outside our borders. Surround our leaders who have been charged with national security with wise counsel. Help them to be men and women of integrity who place the good of this nation above their own, and whose motives are right.

Give our leaders the discernment, understanding, and knowledge concerning the issues of safety for the people of this nation. I pray that Your wisdom interacts with every decision made, and You bring forth actions that are best for our country.

Strengthen our security forces at every level spiritually, mentally, and physically. Give the men and women courage and fortitude to stand strong in the face of adversity. May they be bold and courageous to stand up for what is right, and defy the forces that would come against our country.

I pray for the safety and protection of those who risk their lives for us. May no harm or evil come near them. May they be discerning, wise, and vigilant concerning every aspect of their safety. May Your hand of protection cover them and keep them safe. Lead, guide, and direct them by Your Spirit.

In Jesus' mighty name.

MISSION
AND
SERVICE

Faith and obedience are bound up in the same bundle.

He that obeys God trusts God; and he that trusts God

obeys God. He that is without faith is without works;

and he that is without works is without faith.

—CHARLES H. SPURGEON

If anyone is poor among your fellow Israelites in any of the towns of the land the Lord your God is giving you, do not be hardhearted or tightfisted toward them. . . . There will always be poor people in the land. Therefore I command you to be openhanded toward your fellow Israelites who are poor and needy in your land.

—DEUTERONOMY 15:7,11 NIV

Don't forget to do good and to share what you have with those in need, for such sacrifices are very pleasing to God.

—HEBREWS 13:16 NLT

While women weep, as they do now, I'll fight; while children go hungry, as they do now, I'll fight; while men go to prison, in and out, in and out, as they do now, I'll fight; while there is a drunkard left, while there is a poor lost girl upon the streets, while there remains one dark soul without the light of God, I'll fight; I'll fight to the very end!

—GENERAL WILLIAM BOOTH

I Want to Be a Blessing

Merciful God,

You are an awesome God, full of compassion and kindness. Your love and mercy know no bounds. Your heart is always turned toward those who are hurting and who have serious needs. You are the father of the orphan and the husband of the widow. You give sight to the blind. You have a special place in Your heart for the poor.

I want to do good deeds and help others. I know that my family needs me. But I also know how much it pleases You when I reach out to others who are in need. I ask that You renew in me a heart of compassion and give me the strength to do something about it.

As I share with the needy both my finances and my time, I will remember to praise You for the many blessings You have given me. Open my eyes to the need around the world—and across the street.

In Jesus' name.

*And we know that in all things God works
for the good of those who love him, who have
been called according to his purpose.*
—**ROMANS 8:28** NIV

*"Anyone who wants to be first must be the
very last, and the servant of all."*
—**MARK 9:35** NIV

*In ordinary life we hardly realize that we receive
a great deal more than we give, and that it is
only with gratitude that life becomes rich.*
—**DIETRICH BONHOEFFER**

I Am Bored and Lack Purpose

Creator God,

I want more in my life right now. I confess that I have fallen into a state of boredom—and maybe a little apathy about life. I don't feel like I have a purpose. I know it's not just about discovering what I want to do—but discovering what *You* want me to do!

Help me to move beyond self-sufficiency, self-indulgence, self-gratifaction to serving You. There are so many needs all around me—the fields are ripe for harvest—and I just need to open my eyes to see the many ways I can go above and beyond the normal and living life to the full.

Forgive me for my complacency and self-centeredness. Give me a new vision to see the world as You do. Whether it is being a better spouse, parent, family member, friend—or tutoring or counseling or building homes or serving in a soup kitchen—I pray that I will receive Your power and energy to get out there and make a difference.

Most of all I want Your Spirit at work within me—teaching me what matters in life and then doing something about it. I now know that focusing only on myself isn't the path to fulfillment and happiness. It is in serving You and others that my life takes on meaning.

Thank You for giving me a purpose that is greater than myself.

In Jesus' name.

Whether, then, you eat or drink or whatever you do, do all to the glory of God. Give no offense either to Jews or to Greeks or to the church of God; just as I also please all men in all things, not seeking my own profit but the profit of the many, so that they may be saved.

—1 Corinthians 10:31–33 NASB

I always thank my God as I remember you in my prayers, because I hear about your love for all his holy people and your faith in the Lord Jesus. I pray that your partnership with us in the faith may be effective in deepening your understanding of every good thing we share for the sake of Christ.

—Philemon 1:4–6 NIV

Too many Christians are stuffing themselves with gospel blessings while millions have never had a taste.

—Vance Havner

I Want to Share My Faith

Dear Lord,

Thank You for my salvation. You left Heaven to live among us and show us what a perfect life looks like—and ultimately to die for our sins in order that we might be saved. If I have failed to say it often enough, I want to say now that I am forever grateful for what You have done for me through Your death and resurrection.

I don't want be judgmental of those around me. But I do see friends, family members, and acquaintances who are living without You. Some have made a disaster of their lives. Others seem fine by external measures, but are not prepared for eternity because they don't know You and haven't received You into their lives.

I pray that You would give me a special love for anyone who has not experienced the joy of Your salvation. I pray that You would make what I say and do be a positive witness of knowing You. I know that doesn't mean perfection—only You are perfect—but it does mean a grace-filled life. I pray that You would give me opportunities in everyday life and situations to boldly and comfortably share with others what You have done for me.

The Lord is good to those whose hope is in him,

to the one who seeks him; it is good to wait

quietly for the salvation of the Lord.

—LAMENTATIONS 3:25–26 NIV

May our Lord Jesus Christ himself and God our

Father, who loved us and by his grace gave us eternal

encouragement and good hope, encourage your hearts

and strengthen you in every good deed and word.

—2 THESSALONIANS 2:16–17 NIV

God always gives His best to those who

leave the choice with Him.

—JIM ELLIOTT

I Need Hope for the Future

God of All Wisdom and Knowledge,

The greatest things we can possess in life are faith, hope, and love. Right now I don't feel very hopeful. I confess that no matter how hard I try, I just don't have a sense of optimism about the future. I feel like the world is going in the wrong direction on matters of faith and morality—and it affects everything else negatively from the strength of our nation to the lives of individual families.

Remind me that there never has been and never will be any sure hope other than You. Nations rise and fall. Companies come and go. Neighborhoods change. Fortunes are found and lost. But You are eternal. And Your love for me is constant for now and throughout all eternity, giving me a hope and a future. You came that we should not perish but have eternal life.

Lord, help me to see tomorrow and each future day in light of eternity. Remind me that You have everything under control. If there is evil at work in the world it is only because You are slow to anger and judgment so that more may be saved.

Thank You for planting inside me the seeds of hope and help me nourish those seeds through faith and prayer.

In Jesus' name.

*For it is by grace you have been saved, through faith—
and this is not from yourselves, it is the gift of God—
not by works, so that no one can boast. For we are
God's handiwork, created in Christ Jesus to do good
works, which God prepared in advance for us to do.*

—EPHESIANS 2:8–10 NIV

*But I have raised you up for this very purpose,
that I might show you my power and that my
name might be proclaimed in all the earth.*

—EXODUS 9:16 NIV

*I am only one, but I am one. I cannot do everything,
but I can do something. And I will not let what
I cannot do interfere with what I can do.*

—EDWARD EVERETT HALE

I Want to Make a Difference

Heavenly Father,

You have been at work in my heart. You have planted seeds of love and care that I have never had on my own. I have awoken to the needs of the world both near and far. I am willing and ready to help wherever You want me to serve.

There are so many things that need to be done that I don't know where to begin. I don't know what groups to support financially and I don't know where You want me to get directly involved.

I ask that You would speak to my heart and to my mind on where You want me to serve. Thank You for common sense, for the counsel of others, for opportunities that are immediately in front of me, but I also ask to hear Your voice. To feel Your call on my life. To be empowered by knowing that when I minister to others I am ministering in Your name.

You have planted a seed in my heart and I pray that You would make it into something beautiful, O God.

In Jesus' holy name.

*"For God so loved the world that he gave his only
Son, so that everyone who believes in him will not
perish but have eternal life. God did not send his
Son into the world to condemn it, but to save it."*

—**JOHN 3:16–17** NLT

*"You have heard that it was said, 'Love your neighbor and
hate your enemy.' But I tell you, love your enemies and pray
for those who persecute you, that you may be children of your
Father in heaven. He causes his sun to rise on the evil and the
good, and sends rain on the righteous and the unrighteous."*

—**MATTHEW 5:43–45** NIV

Love means loving the unlovable—or it is no virtue at all.

—**G. K. CHESTERTON**

LOVING MY WORLD

Dear God,

I know that there are so many things happening in the world today that break Your Heart—and that anger You.

As I see reports of violence, cruelty, exploitation, and negligence, I too, get sad and angry—and, oftentimes, judgmental. There are individuals and groups and even countries I don't feel love for. Help me to never make excuses for governments, leaders, and organizations that do what is evil, but do remind me that if Your purpose for sending Jesus is not to condemn the world then that can't be my focus either.

I ask that You help me to be redemptive—to see the world through Your eyes of love and compassion. When I begin to condemn others, help me to pray for the salvation of the wicked instead. Show me ways I can support ministries and organizations that act redemptively in the world—and to participate directly as You provide me opportunity.

In the loving name of Jesus.

Then I heard the voice of the Lord saying,

"Whom shall I send? And who will go for us?"

And I said, "Here am I. Send me!"

—ISAIAH 6:8 NIV

*Then Jesus came to them and said, "All authority in heaven
and on earth has been given to me. Therefore go and make
disciples of all nations, baptizing them in the name of the
Father and of the Son and of the Holy Spirit, and teaching
them to obey everything I have commanded you. And
surely I am with you always, to the very end of the age."*

—MATTHEW 28:18–20 NIV

Preach the gospel at all times; when necessary, use words.

—ST. FRANCIS OF ASSISI

I Feel a Call to Ministry

Loving Father,

I have begun to sense in my heart that You are calling me to commit myself to full time ministry. I know that all Christians are called to be ministers and that I can serve You in whatever place You have put me in life. I know that I can be a student of Your Word and grow in my impact right where I am.

But I also know You ask some people to serve You full time in a church or ministry organization. I pray that if that is Your will for me it will become crystal clear to me. I ask You to give me the courage and obedience to pursue that calling, even if it means a major life change and less money. I pray that I would be ready to sacrifice my current plans to pursue training and preparation to fulfill that call. Even as Your Son did not begin His earthly ministry until He was thirty years old, I ask for the patience to spend the time necessary to be the most effective minister I can be.

Most of all, give me a great vision of You and Your mission for me.

I am honored that You love me and communicate with me. If Your call on my life is to full-time ministry, I will accept with all humility and gratitude, knowing that nothing else will bring me the joy and satisfaction of being in the center of Your will.

In Jesus' holy name.

20 IMPORTANT BIBLE PASSAGES ON PRAYER

1. If my people, who are called by my name, will humble themselves and pray and seek my face and turn from their wicked ways, then I will hear from heaven, and I will forgive their sin and will heal their land. (2 Chronicles 7:14 NIV)

2. Hear me, LORD, my plea is just; listen to my cry. Hear my prayer—it does not rise from deceitful lips. Let my vindication come from you; may your eyes see what is right. Though you probe my heart, though you examine me at night and test me, you will find that I have planned no evil; my mouth has not transgressed. Though people tried to bribe me, I have kept myself from the ways of the violent through what your lips have commanded. My steps have held to your paths; my feet have not stumbled. I call on you, my God, for you will answer me; turn your ear to me and hear my prayer. (Psalm 17:1–6 NIV)

3. "Because he loves me," says the Lord, "I will rescue him; I will protect him, for he acknowledges my name. He will call on me, and I will answer him; I will be with him in trouble, I will deliver

him and honor him. With long life I will satisfy him and show him my salvation." (Psalm 91:14–16 NIV)

4. The sacrifice of the wicked is an abomination, hateful and exceedingly offensive to the Lord, but the prayer of the upright is His delight! (Proverbs 15:8 AMP)

5. Give ear and come to me; listen, that you may live. I will make an everlasting covenant with you, my faithful love promised to David. . . . Seek the LORD while he may be found; call on him while he is near. Let the wicked forsake their ways and the unrighteous their thoughts. Let them turn to the LORD, and he will have mercy on them, and to our God, for he will freely pardon. "For my thoughts are not your thoughts, neither are your ways my ways," declares the LORD. (Isaiah 55:3,6–8 NIV)

6. "You have heard that it was said, 'Love your neighbor and hate your enemy.' But I tell you, love your enemies and pray for those who persecute you, that you may be children of your Father in heaven." (Matthew 5:43–45 NIV)

7. "And when you pray, do not be like the hypocrites, for they love to pray standing in the synagogues and on the street corners to be seen by others. Truly I tell you, they have received their reward in full. But when you pray, go into your room, close the door and pray to your Father, who is unseen. Then your Father, who sees what is done in secret, will reward you. And when you pray, do not keep on babbling like pagans, for they think they will be heard because of their many words. Do not be like them, for your Father knows what you need before you ask him.

"This, then, is how you should pray: 'Our Father in heaven, hallowed be your name, your kingdom come, your will be done, on earth as it is in heaven. Give us today our daily bread. And forgive us our debts, as we also have forgiven our debtors. And lead us not into temptation, but deliver us from the evil one.'" (Matthew 6:5–13 NIV)

8. "Ask and it will be given to you; seek and you will find; knock and the door will be opened to you. For everyone who asks receives; the one who seeks finds; and to the one who knocks, the door will be opened. Which of you, if your son asks for bread, will give him a stone? Or if he asks for a fish, will give him a snake? If you, then, though you are evil, know how to give good gifts to your children, how much more will your Father in heaven give good gifts to those who ask him!" (Matthew 7:7–11 NIV)

9. "Again I say to you that if two of you agree on earth concerning anything that they ask, it will be done for them by My Father in heaven. For where two or three are gathered together in My name, I am there in the midst of them." (Matthew 18:19–20 NKJV)

10. "Watch and pray so that you will not fall into temptation. The spirit is willing, but the flesh is weak." (Matthew 26:41 NIV)

11. "Have faith in God," Jesus answered. "Truly I tell you, if anyone says to this mountain, 'Go, throw yourself into the sea,' and does not doubt in their heart but believes that what they say will happen, it will be done for them. Therefore I tell you, whatever you ask for in prayer, believe that you have received it, and it will be yours. And when you stand praying, if you hold anything against

anyone, forgive them, so that your Father in heaven may forgive you your sins." (Mark 11:22–25 NIV)

12. At Caesarea there was a man named Cornelius, a centurion in what was known as the Italian Regiment. He and all his family were devout and God-fearing; he gave generously to those in need and prayed to God regularly. One day at about three in the afternoon he had a vision. He distinctly saw an angel of God, who came to him and said, "Cornelius!" Cornelius stared at him in fear. "What is it, Lord?" he asked. The angel answered, "Your prayers and gifts to the poor have come up as a memorial offering before God." (Acts 10:1–4 NIV)

13. In the same way, the Spirit helps us in our weakness. We do not know what we ought to pray for, but the Spirit himself intercedes for us through wordless groans. And he who searches our hearts knows the mind of the Spirit, because the Spirit intercedes for God's people in accordance with the will of God. (Romans 8:26–27 NIV)

14. Pray at all times (on every occasion, in every season) in the Spirit, with all [manner of] prayer and entreaty. To that end keep alert and watch with strong purpose and perseverance, interceding in behalf of all the saints (God's consecrated people). (Ephesians 6:18 AMP)

15. Rejoice in the Lord always. I will say it again: Rejoice! Let your gentleness be evident to all. The Lord is near. Do not be anxious about anything, but in every situation, by prayer and petition, with thanksgiving, present your requests to God. And the peace of God,

which transcends all understanding, will guard your hearts and your minds in Christ Jesus. (Philippians 4:4–7 NIV)

16. Be earnest and unwearied and steadfast in your prayer [life], being [both] alert and intent in [your praying] with thanksgiving. (Colossians 4:2 AMP)

17. Be happy [in your faith] and rejoice and be glad-hearted continually (always); be unceasing in prayer [praying perseveringly]; thank [God] in everything [no matter what the circumstances may be, be thankful and give thanks], for this is the will of God for you [who are] in Christ Jesus [the Revealer and Mediator of that will]. (1 Thessalonians 5:16–18 AMP)

18. I urge, then, first of all, that petitions, prayers, intercession and thanksgiving be made for all people—for kings and all those in authority, that we may live peaceful and quiet lives in all godliness and holiness. This is good, and pleases God our Savior, who wants all people to be saved and to come to a knowledge of the truth. . . . Therefore I want the men everywhere to pray, lifting up holy hands without anger or disputing. (1 Timothy 2:1–4,8 NIV)

19. Is anyone among you in trouble? Let them pray. Is anyone happy? Let them sing songs of praise. Is anyone among you sick? Let them call the elders of the church to pray over them and anoint them with oil in the name of the Lord. And the prayer offered in faith will make the sick person well; the Lord will raise them up. If they have sinned, they will be forgiven. Therefore confess your sins to each other and pray for each other so that you

may be healed. The prayer of a righteous person is powerful and effective. (James 5:13–16 NIV)

20. This is the confidence we have in approaching God: that if we ask anything according to his will, he hears us. And if we know that he hears us—whatever we ask—we know that we have what we asked of him. (1 John 5:14–15 NIV)

A QUICK LESSON ON PRAYER

In Luke 11:1, we read that Jesus took His disciples away from the crowds in order to teach them to pray. What this means is that prayer will not always come naturally for you. You will have to practice and grow in your prayer life.

You may not see any results from your prayers as you get started. You may not sense God's presence. But, as you develop your prayer life, you will find that prayer is a great source of power, freedom, and guidance in your life.

Five Elements of Prayer

PRAISE

When we praise God we speak well of Him. We recognize that He created the universe and every living thing in it—including you; that He redeemed us through the blood of Jesus, who died on the Cross and rose again for our sins; that He has never forsaken His promise to love and care for us.

God is all-powerful, all-knowing, good, faithful, and loving. It is no wonder that God wants us to praise Him. Certainly praise brings pleasure to God. But more than that, praise is good for us. It serves as a constant reminder to us of who God is and who we are.

He is the Creator. We are created. Praise is our way of remembering that we are not independent agents. We are dependent on God's continued activity and interest in our lives and in our world. Even if we and everyone else fail to take the time to praise God for who He is, the fact remains that we are dependent upon Him.

In Romans 1:21–23, we read: "For although they knew God, they neither glorified him as God nor gave thanks to him, but their thinking became futile and their foolish hearts were darkened. Although they claimed to be wise, they became fools and exchanged the glory of the immortal God for images made to look like mortal man and birds and animals and reptiles."

In our culture, the worship of "images" is alive and well. These idols are not necessarily made of stone, gold, or silver. But the idols of scientific accomplishment, human understanding, prosperity, technology, and wealth can be seen everywhere.

The foolish continue to worship the created rather than the Creator. When we take time to praise God in our prayer life, we are able to avoid the devastating sin of pride.

THANKSGIVING

For many, Thanksgiving really does come only once a year. We don't live in an overly "thankful" world. Overall, most of us are not as grateful as we should be. We focus on what we don't get rather than what we have been given.

In Psalm 105, we are told to come into God's presence with thanksgiving. In Philippians 4:4–8, we are told to give thanks in all things. We thank God for all that we have and all that He has done for us. We acknowledge that every gift and talent we possess is from God.

Do we thank God even when bad things happen? Do we even thank God for the things about us that we don't like?

According to Philippians 4:6, we are to give thanks in all situations: "but in everything, by prayer and petition, *with thanksgiving*, present your requests to God," (emphasis added).

This does not mean that we are thankful that bad things have happened. We are thankful in spite of them. We focus on the half-full glass, instead of always noting the half-empty glass. We don't blissfully ignore the bad. But even in the worst of situations, we can at least be thankful that God is with us and will never forsake us!

The attitude of thankfulness is of course closely related to praise. The difference is that we praise God for who He is. We thank God for what He has done for us and the many gifts and talents He has given to us.

CONFESSION

One of the hardest things to do is to admit failure.

I was wrong. I blew it. I messed up. I sinned.

Imagine the humiliation that David experienced when he confessed to his adulterous affair with Bathsheba and the way he had her husband killed to cover it up. In Psalm 51, David cried out in real agony as he acknowledged that he had sinned against God and man. In the same way, when face-to-face with the realization of his sinfulness, Isaiah fell to his face and cried, "Woe is me!" (6:5 KJV).

Confession is not just good for the soul. Confession is essential to maintaining a relationship with God. It cannot be left out of our prayer life. With David, we acknowledge any sin against God and others. We ask forgiveness. In doing so, we acknowledge the seriousness of sin. We are chastened. We are motivated not to sin anymore. We are cleansed, so that we can continue our fellowship with God.

Have you had a time in your life like David? Do you have any unresolved sin in your life? Are there some ways that you are falling short of all that God wants you to be? Why don't you acknowledge this simply and briefly right now.

PETITIONS

We are told to take everything to God in prayer, including our needs and wants. Keep in mind . . . God desires that we bring our requests to Him. James says, "You do not have, because you do not ask God," (4:2). Just as a parent desires to know his child's needs, so God wants us to bring our needs before Him.

Our ultimate prayer is like that of Jesus in the garden: "Not my will, but thine." This reminder serves as a major deterrent to praying selfishly and from wrong motives. It is again James who tells us, "When you ask, you do not receive, because you ask with wrong motives," (4:3). When we tell God, "Not my will, but your will be done," we will keep our motives on track.

Sometimes God answers, "No." I would like to give my children everything they desire. However, I would not be a responsible parent if I were to do so. Some things are harmful for them, other things they are not ready for. For that reason, God sometimes does not grant our requests. As you bring your requests to God, keep in mind that He sees more than you do. Be willing to withdraw and change your requests as you sense God saying no to what you have brought before Him.

Sometimes God answers in a manner different than we expect. Part of having faith is having a confident expectancy. That is great. However, don't let this expectancy turn into inflexible expectations of just how God is to answer your prayers. He probably has a better way to answer your prayer than you could ever think of!

Sometimes we have to wait for answers. We definitely live in a *now* society. Fast-food restaurants ensure that you have your food immediately. Once you are out on your own and making money, credit card companies will work with you so that you can have any gadget or gizmo you want right now—whether or not you can afford it.

Your needs will be met. Jesus reminds His disciples in the Sermon on the Mount that there is no need to worry about the basic needs of life: "Look at the birds of the air; they do not sow or reap or store away in barns, and yet your heavenly Father feeds them. Are you not much more valuable than they?" (Matthew 6:26). This is no call to irresponsibility. It is a reminder of God's continued concern for our lives. He knows our needs and will supply them.

Don't be surprised when God does answer your prayers! Have you every prayed for something, seen it happen, and then not given God the credit? "Maybe it was a coincidence!" One person has noted that "coincidences" always occurred much more often in his life when he prayed than when he didn't pray. Don't be surprised by some "coincidences" in your life that look like answers to prayer.

Don't forget to thank God for answers to your prayers. You may need to reread the "Thanksgiving" section of this chapter several more times before you get the hang of it. We need to constantly remind ourselves to thank God for what He is doing in our lives. In Luke 17:11–19, ten lepers were healed by Jesus. How many remembered to give Him thanks? Only one. You may be in the minority, but it seems only right to be a person who remembers to say, "Thanks, Jesus."

INTERCESSION

There is a special kind of prayer called "intercession." What happens in intercessory prayer is that we go before God on behalf of someone else. Often, intercession is for someone who is not a Christian and who will not pray for himself.

This is what makes intercessory prayer so hard to understand. We know that everyone is responsible for his own life before God. No one can force someone else to become a Christian, and God will not force anyone to do so either. However, when we intercede in prayer for someone else, special conviction and awareness of God can take place in that person's life. The Holy Spirit will communicate to that person in a more intense way just because we prayed. The major factor is not his faithfulness but your—the intercessor's—faithfulness.

We can also intercede for people when they are ill; when they are facing trials and tribulations; when they are going through any situation where they need the extra support of other Christians. Intercession is, for many, a powerful ministry. But it is not easy. It takes steadfast persistence, stretching faith, tears and deep feelings for the person, and often fasting and the help of others uniting with you in prayer.

We can't forget that, particularly when we are praying for someone's salvation, God will not violate that person's free will. He has given everyone the choice to live for or against him. What you can do is bombard him in such a way that he is keenly aware of God's presence. That person alone determines how he will respond to such an awareness of God.

PRAY WITHOUT CEASING

Prayer needs to be a habit that is cultivated as an ongoing process and force in your life. Put reminders for yourself in your books, in your pockets, on your clothing, in your room, so that prayer will be a conversation with God throughout your day. Get in the habit of offering short prayers to God all day long.

YOUR ATTITUDE IN PRAYER

Proper reverence for God is always a must. The first four of the Ten Commandments give us guidance for the proper honor and respect we are to show to our Heavenly Father. For example, we are not to take God's name in vain—that is, use it lightly.

But we should also note that in Romans 8:15, Paul tells us that we can call on God as "Abba, Father." Abba simply means *Daddy*. God is not some distant ruler who wishes us to grovel before Him. He is a loving "Daddy."

You can come to God in prayer with the same familiarity as if you were going to an earthly father who was very gentle and loving. You do not have to pray in Elizabethan English. You can talk to Him in the same way you would talk to your best friend, using the same type of words and voice. This is not a sign of disrespect, but it is our way of accepting God's invitation to be a part of His immediate family.

SCRIPTURE
INDEX

PROVERBS

ECCLESIASTES

SONG OF SOLOMON

Isaiah

Jeremiah

Lamentations

Daniel

Joel

Micah

Nahum

Zechariah

Malachi

Matthew

Mark

Ephesians

Philippians

Colossians